The Peter and Paul

(ST PETERSBURG)

Fortress

A CULTURAL GUIDE

AURORA ART PUBLISHERS
LENINGRAD

The Peter and Paul (ST PETERSBURG) Fortress

Compiled and introduced by Constantine Logachev
Translated from the Russian by Kathleen Carroll
Designed by Alexander Lobanov

Printed and bound in the USSR

П $\frac{4902020000\text{-}826}{023(01)\text{-}89}$ 3-89

ISBN 5-7300-0085-5

The author expresses thanks to the following organizations for their assistance in the compilation of textual and illustrative documentary materials for this publication: the Library of the USSR Academy of Sciences, Leningrad; the Leningrad Branch of the Archives of the USSR Academy of Sciences; the Saltykov-Shchedrin Public Library, Leningrad; the Central Historical Archives of the USSR, Leningrad; the Central Archives of the Film-, Phono- and Photo-documents, Leningrad; the Hermitage Museum, Leningrad; the Russian Museum, Leningrad; the Military-Historical Museum of Artillery, Engineering and Communication Forces, Leningrad; the Museum of the History of Leningrad; the State Inspection Board for the Protection of Monuments under the Head Office of Architecture and Design of the Leningrad City Executive Committee. The author also thanks Yuri M. Denisov for his help.

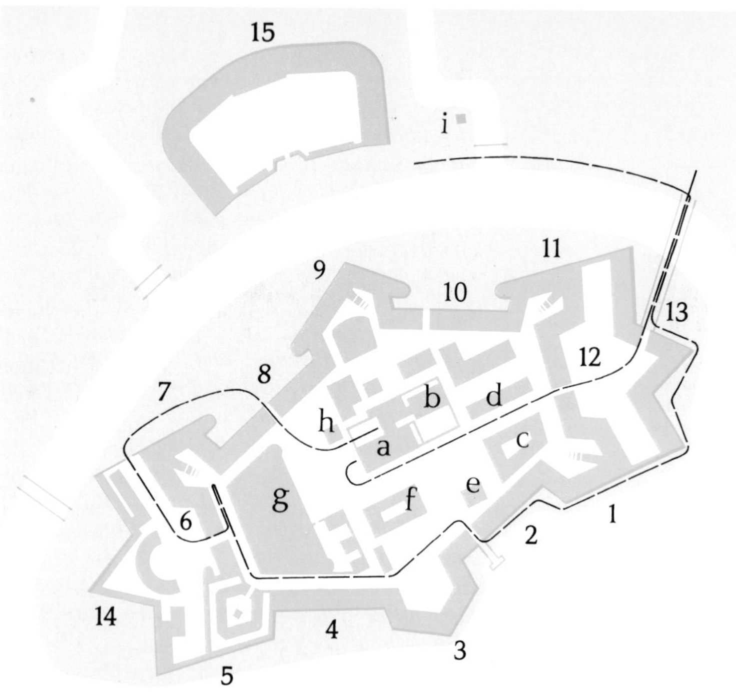

a The Sts Peter and Paul Cathedral
b The Grand Ducal Burial Vault
c The Engineers' House
d The Artillery Warehouse
e The Main Guardhouse
f The Commandant's House
g The Mint Works
h The Boathouse
i Monument on the supposed place of the execution of the Decembrists
1 The Tsar Bastion (Bastion of Peter I) with the ramp
2 The Neva Curtain Wall with the Neva Gate
3 The Naryshkin Bastion (St Catherine Bastion, the Empress Catherine I Bastion) with the flagstaff tower
4 The St Catherine Curtain Wall
5 The Trubetskoi Bastion with the building of prison
6 The Vasilyevsky Island Curtain Wall with the Vasilyevsky Island Gate
7 The Zotov Bastion with the ramp
8 The St Nicholas Curtain Wall with the St Nicholas (Second Kronwerk) Gate
9 The Golovkin Bastion (Bastion of St Anne, the Empress Anna Bastion)
10 The Kronwerk Curtain Wall with the Kronwerk (First Kronwerk) Gate
11 The Menshikov Bastion (Bastion of Peter II) with the ramp
12 The St Peter Curtain Wall with the St Peter Gate
13 The St John (Ioannovsky) Ravelin with the St John Gate, half-counterguards and batardeau, and the St John (St Peter) Bridge leading to the gate
14 The St Alexei (Alexeyevsky) Ravelin with the half-counterguards and batardeau, and with the building of archives
15 The kronwerk with the Defence Arsenal

The Peter and Paul (St Petersburg) Fortress is the historical nucleus of the City on the Neva as well as one of its most interesting and beautiful architectural complexes. From as far away as the Gulf of Finland one can see the distant gilded spire of the fortress cathedral, one of the main features of the Leningrad skyline.

fortress — a type of permanent fortified structure (built of strong materials and serving as a means of defence during battle), the most essential and fundamental part of the fortress is the main rampart (an enclosed fence containing gate openings)

bastion fortification system — a method of building a fortress in which the main rampart consists of so-called bastion fronts (segments comprised of curtain walls and two adjacent demi-bastions)

The Peter and Paul Fortress is the only surviving permanent fortified structure in the Soviet Union planned and executed in strict accordance with the so-called bastion fortification system. Even in Western Europe only a few citadels built according to the same principles remain which are as well preserved as the fortress in Leningrad (for example, analogous structures at Lucca in Italy, Perpignan in France and Valletta in Malta). The main gate of the fortress on the Neva, the Sts Peter and Paul Cathedral, the Mint Works, the Defence Arsenal and other structures on its territory rank among the most interesting architectural landmarks of the eighteenth to the early twentieth century. In addition, the fortress is closely tied with great military, political and cultural events, important not only in the history of St Petersburg/Petrograd/Leningrad, but in the history of the entire country: the Northern War, the assimilation of lands along the banks of the Neva, which in the eighteenth century were called "New Russian America", the Decembrist Uprising, the social movement of the intelligentsia, the victory of the October Revolution of 1917, the War of 1941—45...

The present guide will provide the reader with basic information about this unique cultural and historical complex. The description will be exclusively based on sources directly illuminating its almost 300-year history.

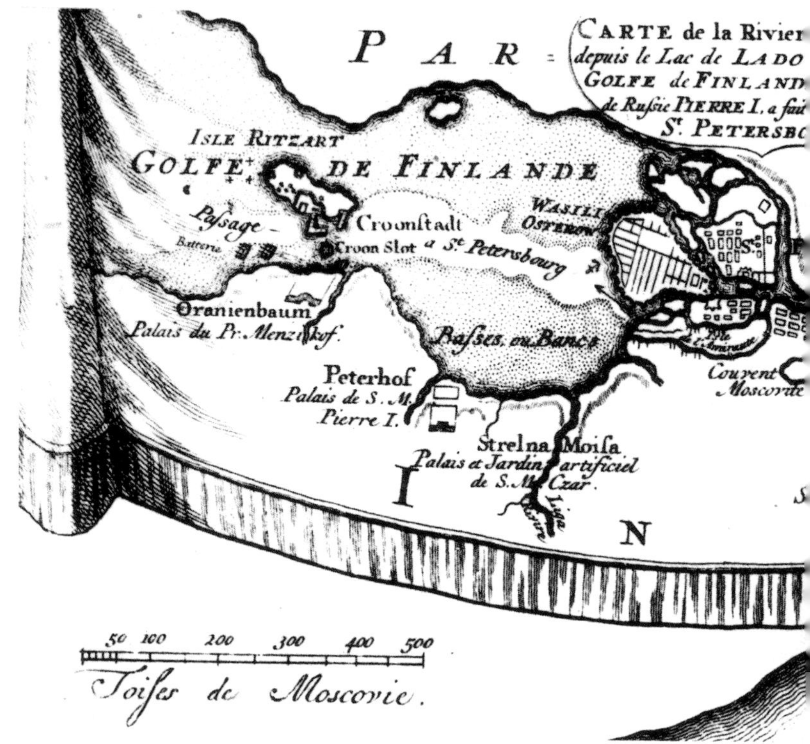

Map of the River Neva from Lake Ladoga to the Gulf of Finland, Where the Russian Emperor Peter I Ordered the City St Petersburg Be Built; placed in the upper left corner of the engraving *Map of the City and Fortification of St Petersburg, New Capital and Residence of the Russian Emperors, Built by the Emperor Peter I on Several Islands in the Gulf of Finland at the South of the River Neva* (map published in Amsterdam in the beginning of the 1720s). In the right-hand part of the map at the source of the Neva, the notation:

In 1617 Sweden completely closed off Russia's access to the Baltic Sea by annexing territories to the south and north of the Neva, i.e., the Izhora Land (Ingria or Ingermanland) and Karelia. In 1699 a Russian-Danish-Saxon anti-Swedish coalition was organized. In February 1700 Saxony declared war against Sweden. In March Denmark did the same, and in August Russia followed suit. Later on Poland, Prussia, Hannover, Mecklenburg and Turkey also partook in this war, which became known as the Northern War.

In October 1702 Russia stormed the island at the source of the Neva, and took the Swedish fortress Nöteburg, which had been founded under the name of Oreshek (the

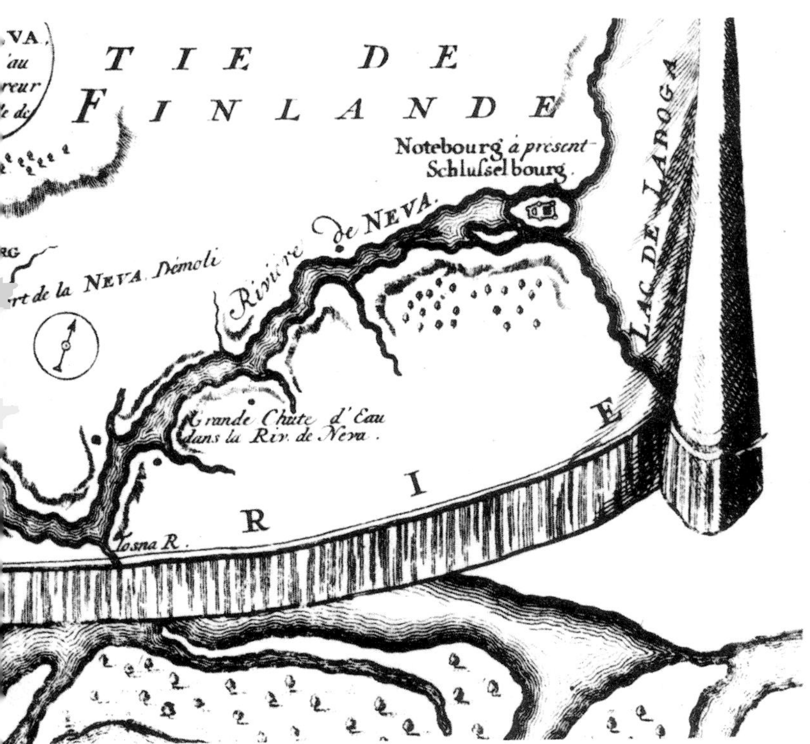

Nöteburg, now Schlüsselburg; in the centre, on the right bank of the Neva, before St Petersburg, not far from the beginning of the Neva delta, the notation: *Fortification on the Neva now destroyed* (that is, Nyenskans); to the left, in the Gulf of Finland, between two shoals, the indication: *Passage to St Petersburg*, and this passage is guarded on the south by a battery and Crohn-Schlott, and on the north by Kronstadt (The Russian Museum, Leningrad)

Nut) in 1323 by the people of Novgorod. In April 1703 from this fortress, now called Schlüsselburg, a campaign was launched downstream along the Neva under the command of Field-marshal Boris Sheremetev, one of the closest associates of Tsar Piotr Alexeyevich (Peter I called the Great). At this time the Tsar wrote Sheremetev the following: "Time, time, time. Don't give the enemy a chance to anticipate us."

Moving quickly to the west, at the end of April Russian forces sieged the fortress Nyenskans, built by the Swedes a little above the Neva delta, on a cape at the confluence of the Neva and its largest right-wing tributary, the Okhta. By May 1 Nyenskans had surrendered

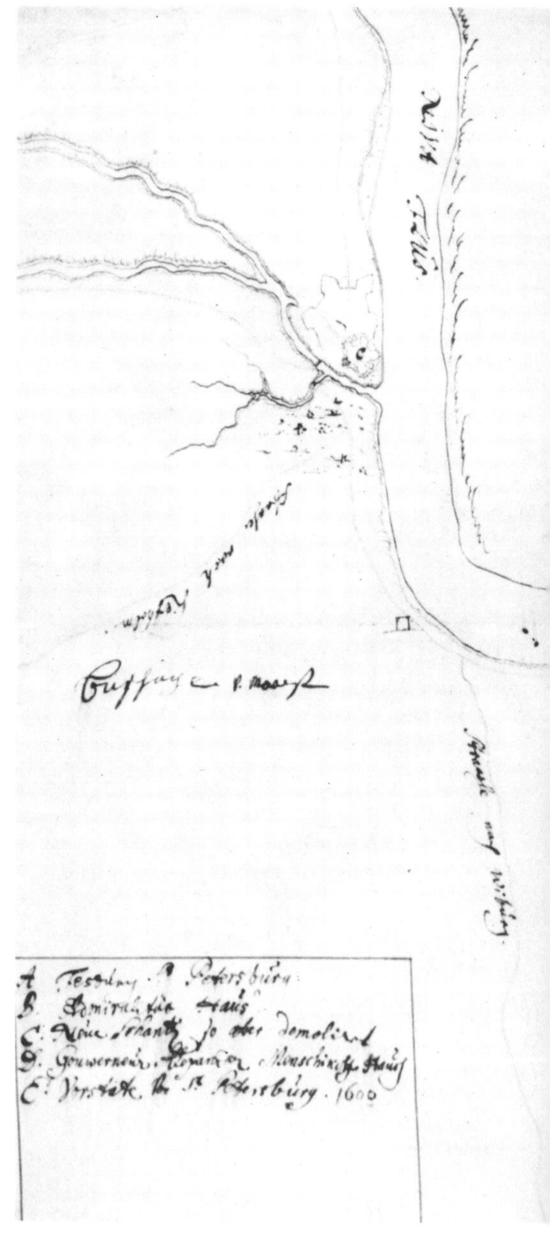

Map of the Neva delta believed to have been drawn in 1705 with the title on the back side: *Islands of Petersburg and Currents of the Neva as far as Nyenskans*. The map is arranged so that its lower edge corresponds to the northern part of the actual locality. Thus, the Gulf of Finland is at the right. The capitalized Latin letters on the map indicate: A — the St Petersburg Fortress, B — the Admiralty buildings, C — the ruins of Nyenskans, D — House of Governor Alexander Menshikov, EEE — the suburbs of St Petersburg located to the east and north-east of the fortress (Library of the USSR Academy of Sciences, Leningrad)

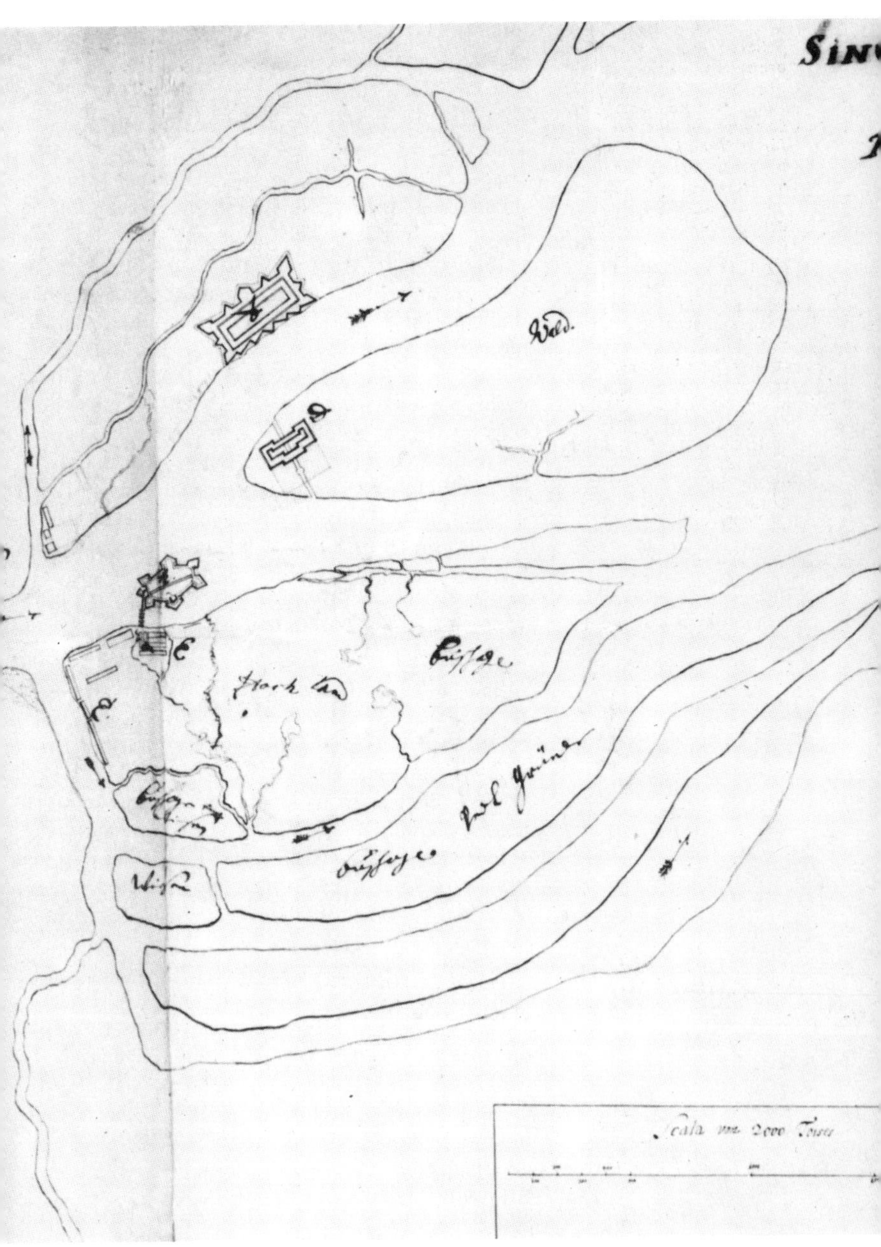
Wald.

and was immediately renamed Schlottburg. On May 7 the Swedish squadron, standing at the Neva Inlet near the mouth of the Bolshaya (Large) Neva, was attacked by a Russian detachment equipped only with simple boats. The Swedish fleet, which formerly had maintained complete dominion over the Baltic, lost two frigates. This was the first naval victory in the history of Russia.

In order to consolidate Russia's position on the Gulf of Finland, a military council summoned by Peter the Great made the decision not to reinforce Schlottburg, but rather to build a new fortress nearer to the sea at a point which could be defended by means of natural barriers better than at the cape formed by the Neva and Okhta. Soon thereafter a small island was selected for this purpose located on the Neva delta to the west of Schlottburg and named "het Mooiste Lust Eiland" — "the Happiest Island", the name coming from the Dutch as Peter the Great was fond of that language. After the construction of a fortress which occupied the entire island, it remained without an official name until the end of the eighteenth century. In the nineteenth and early twentieth centuries it was called Fortress Island, and subsequently received the name it bears today — Zayachy (Hare) Island, which is the translation of the name given the island by the Finnish-speaking portion of the local population in the seventeenth century.

The new fortress, whose construction of wood and earth was begun already in May 1703, soon became the centre of Russia's activities on the Neva delta and, at the same time, the main stronghold of the Russian army in Ingria. The architect of the fortress is unknown. Some scholars suggest that it was designed by the French engineer Joseph Gaspard Lambert, a participant in the Neva campaign.

On June 29, 1703, a small wooden church was dedicated to the Apostles Peter and Paul in the centre of the unfinished fortress, and the fortress itself was named in the Dutch manner — St Pietersburg. Very quickly the short form of the name came into use, Pietersburg, as well as the names pronounced in the German manner, St Petersburg and Petersburg.

Europeans followed attentively the swift movements of the Russian troops and, of course, well understood Peter's intentions. The European press printed a whole line of news about the events on the Neva delta. This information was translated and circulated regularly in the first Russian newspaper *Vedomosti*, which began to be published on January 2, 1703, in Moscow.

On August 24 *Vedomosti* published a report from Riga about how Peter the Great "...has commanded that a city and fortress be built right on the sea not far from Schlottburg, so that in the future all goods destined for Riga, Narva and Schantz [Nyenskans] could find harbour there, and Persian and Chinese goods would come in there as well". Finally, on October 4, the readers of *Vedomosti* were informed of the following in a report from Riga: "His Royal Highness, upon taking Schlottburg, ordered that a new and excellent fortress be built on an island one mile from the former in the direction of the Eastern [Baltic] Sea. The fortress is to consist of six bastions constructed by 20,000 labourers and to be named in honour of the ruler himself — Petersburg." It is interesting to note that the way the city was named is explained in precisely the same way in both the famous *Dictionnaire universel de commerce* (1723) by the French lawyer and economist Jacques Savary (called Savary des Bruslons) and in the *Concise Synoptic Description of St Petersburg* by Andrei Bogdanov, the first Russian description of the newly built city.

Map of the earthen St Petersburg Fortress — detail of the map *Petersburg Island and Currents of the Neva as far as Nyenskans.* The lower edge of the detailed drawing corresponds to the northern direction of the actual locality (Library of the USSR Academy of Sciences, Leningrad)

Detail of the engraving *St Petersburg* representing the St Petersburg Fortress as it looked in 1704. One can easily make out the ravelin in front of the fortress gate, the Tsar Bastion (above which the flag is flying), the Naryshkin Bastion, the Trubetskoi Bastion, two curtain walls extending along the Neva, the upper part of the wooden fortress cathedral crowned with a tall spire and the roofs of several wooden houses standing in line with it. Behind the fortress a part of the nearby big island can be seen on which stand the first structures of the new city (The Saltykov-Shchedrin Public Library, Leningrad)

Throughout almost the entire summer of 1703 the weather on the Neva delta was very cold and windy and the swampy islands on the river seemed even more damp than usual. Scurvy raged in the Russian camp. The Swedish forces held the mouth of the Neva within the sights of their guns until October. Nevertheless, work on "het Mooiste Lust Eiland" did not stop for a single day. As early as September it was possible to transfer the general headquarters and main Russian military camp from Schlottburg and establish it within the protective walls of the new fortress located on the big island nearby.

As soon as the Swedish war ships left for their winter harbour at Vyborg, Peter the Great embarked for the long island of Kotlin located in the Gulf of Finland at the entrance to the Neva Inlet. Near its eastern end (where subsequently the fortress city of Kronstadt was built) he chose the site for construction of a fort which was to become the "naval lock" of the Neva mouth (in the early eighteenth century the latter was considered to be located right near Kotlin).

History of the fortress

Erected in less than one year, the earthen St Petersburg Fortress took the shape of a multi-angled rampart, closed on all sides, with defensive bastions, a design which incorporated elements of all the then major Western European fortification systems: French, Dutch and German. And this is not surprising since in the beginning of the eighteenth century Russian engineers were familiar with the original works of the most prominent European military engineers, the Frenchman Sébastien Leprestre de Vauban, the Dutchman Menno van Coehoorn, and the German Georg von Rimpler. In 1709 and 1710 the major essays of Coehoorn appeared in Russia in translation under the title *New Fortified Structures Built on Wet or Low Lands ... the Manner in Which It Is Proper to Build a Fortress Today on the Sea or on Rivers*. Somewhat later there appeared the Russian translations of the essays of Rimpler and Vauban.

bastion — the part of the main rampart protruding forward, joined to two neighbouring curtain walls (portions of the main rampart made up of straight walls joining two neighbouring bastions); the bastion is pentagonal in shape and usually consists of four solid walls — two faces (walls, facing the field for the purpose of shooting at the enemy located there) and two flanks (walls facing the space directly in front of the curtain wall for the purpose of shooting at the enemy from embrasures or loopholes if he has succeeded in approaching the curtain wall)

bastion point (exterior corner) — the corner facing the field and created by two adjoining faces of a bastion

The St Petersburg Fortress consisted of six bastions and six curtain walls. Its overall plan — an irregular hexagon with bastion points at each exterior corner — followed the approximate contour of the island from east to west. Three of the six bastions stood on its southern bank, lapped by the waves of the Neva, the other three, on its northern shore, were protected by a small fork of the Neva.

Peter the Great personally observed the erection of one of the three southern bastions, the one which is situated higher than the other two on the Neva, and which was named the Tsar Bastion. The Tsar delegated the task of observing the erection of the remaining five bastions to five of his closest associates, and the bastions were named after each one correspondingly: the central southern was called the Naryshkin Bastion; the lower southern, the Trubetskoi Bastion; the lower northern,

SINUS
INNICUS
Ins: Kalmes
Ins: Wangator
Ins: Pister
Ins: Sowisten
Inf: Seeskar
Inf: Landswenfar
Rikala
Chaskelja
Walkjur
Kiskala
Kuren
Vmat
Achtiala
Chumaljuk
Kaki
Ralikala
R. Rockala
Rukkola
Nivka
Kappel
Akpone
L. Makula
Kopipala
Murila
R. Taracala
Karilagei
Tarkala
Sowasten
Tawala
Antona
Ruki
Kalisch
Repino
Larescheno
Lokowo
Tarkala
Soikina
Garbola
Kochwala
Lannista
Konna
L. Peloe
Gakala
Ditinska
Karowin
Strupowo
Roxa
Nowaja
Polutzie
L. Kabala
Pawlonsko
Itowska
L. Sidatzie
Glubo
Mukowo
L. Leontie
Pilowa
Babina
Dumascheska
Sarga
Gluboko
Biakala
Koporie
Utwerdin
Dolgoe
Pawlowo
Podmoschie
Klimentino
Arbala
Udasala
Rudnelia
Lonoska
Nosdrino
Karpow
Wrewska
Tawastino
Kirstowa
Apolie
Chotini
Ranqorki
Sola
Polska
R. Narowa
Narva
I
N
L
A

L: Roka
Walima
Argolja
Kapel
L. Wulki
Korowala
Lemitela
Ingila
R. Balka
L. Lenia
Rasula
Palkiela
Korgola
Goiht
Korla
Raud
E
L
I
A
Peglast
R. Watta
Kauxema
Libolja
Randakolja
Konzelga
L. Konzelga
Turlina
Pelkelja
Lembolja
Mjaki
Mieljus
R. Sarraka
Puskilja
Korpolja
Limbela
Polweselga
Lidula
Tarilos
Kurkela
Kuiwa
Woli
Gorbolja
Maxa
Kuiwaschki
Wolkowa
Kaugulja
Gimolowa
Kuplalas
Puchtula
Chabala
Alakala
Kakkala
Kokala
Rossiskie towari
Toxa
Morja
Susterbeck
Sestrorezkie Sawodi
Lisej Nos
Pargola
Dupki
Mistula
Ewajarwi
Murino
Rjabowo
Inf. Kostlia
Dubki
Lachta
Kronslot
S. PETERSBURG
Catharinenhof
Annenhof
Mjaka
Porochowie
Sawodi als Figlinæ
Kobiljakowa
Alexander Schanz
Selzo
Bor
R. Schernow
Wirkilja
Posad
Sinjawina
Figlinæ laterariæ
Manuschkina
Koltischi
Newa
Urusowa
Dubrowka
Wogriselka
Petruschcino
Gorlowka
Ribaczja
Slowjanka
Ischora
Peterhof
Strelina
Oranienbaum
Rapola
Aguzulia
Lappala
Gostilizka
Scherebiala
Saborozka
Gluchowa
Biatlizi
Ribovizi
Cosina Nova
S. Krasnoe
R. Ropscha
Duderowa
L. Duderowo
Schungurowo
Pawlouska
Petensko
Cipen
E
R
M
A
Sarskaia
Sloweiaskaia
Slowjanka
Schuchonska
Ischora
Tunina
Moisalskaja
Tosna
Villa Golowina
Figlinæ laterariæ
Pesina
Lesja
Turischkino
Kamenna lomca
Iglino
Rikunowa
Nezerpet
Belaia
Bistina
Kotino
Pudost
Gatzinskaia
Kolpina
Kolodizi
Smolkowo
Gubanizi
Gorka
Greblowo
Ilkino
Kotomaki
Antelewi
Tschorskaja
Fedorowskaja
Tamelia
Samoris
Poderlits
Sunda Sudna
Elizo
Napogi
Kowizow
Serkina
Lisinska
Skworizka
Sdilizka
Abonizi
Glumizi
Donez
Gorka
Kiw
N
D
I
A
Via indirecta
Sloboda Tosna, als Colonia ad Tosnam

ravelin — an exterior auxiliary fortress structure in the shape of a triangle consisting of two wall-legs and erected immediately before a curtain wall

cavalier — an internal auxiliary fortress structure erected within a bastion, and taller than it, which provides for circular fire on the area immediately before the bastion

←

Portion of the engraved map entitled *New and Accurate Drawing of Ingria and Karelia with the Major Portion of the Gulf of Finland and Lake Ladoga, Including Islands In-between* (the map was published in one of the atlases of the famous Augsburg cartographers of the first half of the 18th century, M. Soitter). St Petersburg, situated at the mouth of the Neva, is shown here as a large city. The Gulf of Finland is full of ships (The Russian Museum, Leningrad)

the Zotov Bastion; the central northern, the Golovkin Bastion; and the upper northern, the Menshikov Bastion. Along the length of the island a narrow canal was dug to supply the garrison with water in case of siege. In the curtain wall connecting the Tsar and Menshikov Bastions, the main gate was built, the approach to which was protected by a transversal moat and a ravelin. A pontoon bridge was installed between the small gate in the left face of the ravelin and the large island across the fork of the Neva and named the Krasny (Red or Beautiful) Bridge. The fork itself served as the main docks for military vessels for more than ten years. The cavalier was built in the Golovkin Bastion. Inside the fortress several other buildings for military use were erected as well, and in addition to these a small wooden Lutheran Church of St Anne, which stood on the site until 1710.

On May 7, 1704, exactly one year after the naval victory near the mouth of the Large Neva, Peter the Great again arrived at Kotlin Island, and with a three-day ceremony marked the completion of construction of the fort Crohn-Schlott, whose guns reigned over the fairway near the southern shore of the island. One of Peter's close associates, Alexander Kikin wrote him a humorous account of the commander of the Swedish fleet who "acted very wisely in deciding to leave this place for good last year." At last an access had been opened for Russia onto the vast expanses of the sea, although there remained more than seventeen exhausting years of battle before ultimately securing it by means of a peace treaty with Sweden.

Crohn-Schlott became a reliable guard for the sea approaches to the Neva delta. And the delta itself was protected by the earthen St Petersburg Fortress. On May 14, 1704, the first gun salute from the walls of the new fortress took place in honour of the Russian victory on Lake Peipus, and served as well to mark the end of its construction.

Under the protection of St Petersburg, on the site to which the Russian military camp had been transferred from Schlottburg in the autumn of 1703, a new Russian city began to grow. It took on the names St Pietersburg (Pietersburg) and St Petersburg (Petersburg), but early on the city received the popular nickname "Piter". Accordingly, the big island, on which the main part of the new city was originally situated, came to be called St Petersburg (Petersburg) Island. Today the island is called Petrogradsky from the name "Petrograd" which the city officially received in 1914, after the start of World War I. Since 1710 the fortress itself was officially called the St Petersburg (Petersburg) Fortress. With time it also gained unofficial names such as the "Peter and Paul Fortress" after the cathedral located in its centre.

History of the fortress

As reported on July 22, 1705, in the Moscow newspaper *Vedomosti*, on May 16 in Vyborg a captured Russian captain "alleged that the St Petersburg Fortress was well fortified and could therefore be regarded as the main fortress." In June the Swedish Lieutenant-General Georg Johan Maydell made an attempt to seize the fortress from the north. Although this attempt was successfully repulsed, it was decided to additionally reinforce the northern side of the St Petersburg Fortress. For this purpose from 1705 to 1708 on St Petersburg Island, opposite the Golovkin Bastion, an earthen sod-covered fortification, called *kronwerk*, was erected with an artificial protective slope, *glacis*, around it. In connection with the construction of the kronwerk, the Neva channel, which divided "het Mooiste Lust Eiland" from St Petersburg Island, received the name of Kronwerk Strait.

kronwerk — an auxiliary exterior fortress structure erected immediately in front of the main rampart and consisting of one bastion and two curtains, two demi-bastions, two wings and two winged flanks;
wing — the portion of a kronwerk made up of a straight wall joining the leg of a demi-bastion and a winged flank;
winged flank — the portion of a kronwerk made up of an "L"-shaped wall which unites the wing with the leg of a demi-bastion

glacis — the area around the exterior of the fortress walls which is left without buildings or vegetation in order to deprive the approaching enemy of any possible means of cover

In 1706, in efforts to further reinforce the citadel, work was begun on its complete reconstruction in stone starting with its northern side, the approaches to which were the most vulnerable. The reconstruction was directed by the architect Domenico Trezzini, a Swiss-Italian who started to work in St Petersburg in 1703 along with many other foreign architects and engineers. For the new city, which was destined to become the embodiment of the new Russia, Trezzini drew up plans for numerous palaces, churches, buildings for various organizations and private homes, and nearly all of these projects were actually realized.

On May 3, 1706, work commenced on the stone Menshikov Bastion. But after a mere two and a half months, work was unexpectedly halted: on July 18 fire broke out in the fortress. Miraculously, the fortress escaped irreparable damage; the fire was brought under control before reaching the main powder supply, which was held in wooden casemates within

casemate — a room within a wall of a permanent fortified structure

its earthen walls. Otherwise, the entire fortress would have gone up in smoke. By the end of that building season, workers had succeeded in replacing only the left flank and orillon in stone.

orillon — a short wall facing the field protruding from the bastion's shoulder corner (corner between a face and a flank) for the purpose of covering the flank

In the following year, 1707, the left flank and the orillon of the Golovkin Bastion, as well as the right flank along with the orillon of the Zotov Bastion were reconstructed in stone. In the same year Peter the Great ordered the main gate of the fortress, which was located in the curtain wall joining the Tsar and Menshikov Bastions, be formally decorated.

In 1708 work was undertaken to rebuild the Trubetskoi Bastion in stone. However, once again, at the end of August, all construction work was halted: the Swedish cavalry, under the command of General-Major Georg Lybecker, was advancing on St Petersburg. Having successfully crossed the Neva approximately twenty miles above its delta, Lybecker intended to attack the city from the south. For several weeks the fortress maintained full battle alert, all of the available

The orillon (left) and left flank (centre, behind the tree) of the Menshikov Bastion. The stone reconstruction of the earthen St Petersburg Fortress began here on May 3, 1706

Detail of the 1725 drawing *View of the St Petersburg Fortress with a Portion of the City*, representing the fortress from the southwest. At the left, the Trubetskoi Bastion is visible with a flagstaff and windmill; at the right is the Peter I Bastion behind which can be seen the upper part of the St Peter Gate. Between the two bastions are two curtain walls facing the Neva, and the large opening between them is the site where the stone St Catherine Bastion is being installed. The Sts Peter and Paul Cathedral is still unfinished; yet to be added are the drum and cupola above its eastern section (Library of the USSR Academy of Sciences, Leningrad)

supplies of grain in the vicinity having been hauled into it. To the south of the Neva additional fortifications were hastily built. But once again the Swedes' approach was thwarted.

In June 1709 the Poltava Battle took place, and in June 1710 Russian forces successfully completed the most difficult operation of the Northern War — the siege of Vyborg. Afterwards Peter the Great announced that thanks to taking possession of Vyborg the fortress and city on the Neva delta were finally guaranteed their safety. But at that time these were nothing more than encouraging words. There remained not a few battles to be fought before attaining total security. In the next year, 1711, rebuilding of the fortress in stone was resumed with the next bastion in line, the Tsar Bastion.

In actual fact only after July 1714 when the Russian forces won their first major naval victory of the Northern War near the Hangö (today Hanko) Peninsula at the entrance to the Gulf of Finland, two days after which

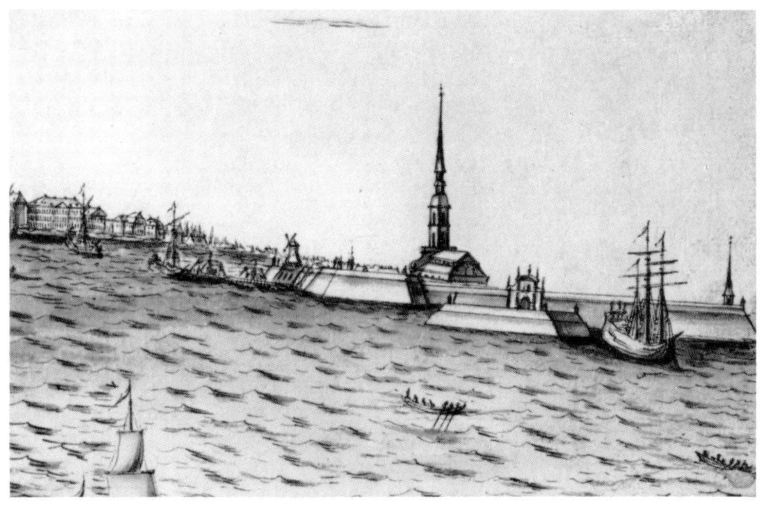

Detail of the 1725 drawing *The Bank Opposite the Fortress* representing the St Petersburg Fortress from the east. The drawing provides a good view of the St Peter Curtain Wall with the St Peter Gate and its corresponding ravelin. The wooden pier on the Neva can be seen on the spot where later the stone St Catherine Bastion was erected, as well as the Trubetskoi Bastion with windmill and the as yet unfinished cathedral lacking drum and cupola over its eastern section (Library of the USSR Academy of Sciences, Leningrad)

they took the Nyslott fortress (Savonlinna), the last stronghold of the Swedes in southern Finland — only then could Peter the Great feel truly secure in his position on the banks of the Neva. (And it is no coincidence that the first triumphal arches were erected in St Petersburg only in the summer of that year.) Beginning at this time the main emphasis was switched from rebuilding the bastions and curtain walls of the fortress to finishing, according to the plans of the architect Trezzini, the new stone Cathedral of Sts Peter and Paul, the construction of which had begun in 1712. At this time Peter required above all "that an allotment be made for a clock in the belltower." In 1717 work was begun on aesthetic improvements of the main gate of the fortress. The gate received the name of St Peter, after the statue of the Apostle Peter which was installed above it; and the curtain wall in which the gate was located also received the name of St Peter.

On September 4, 1721, precisely at noon, twenty-one cannon shots rang out from the walls of the fortress; and at three p.m. in the company of two trumpeters, a kettle-drummer and six grenadiers, a guard-lieutenant drove out of the St Peter Gate holding a white banner which bore two laurel branches under a wreath. They announced to the people of St Petersburg the end of the twenty-one-year Northern War. With the signing of the Nystad Peace treaty the Neva delta and surrounding territories were formally returned to Russia.

Now there was less impetus than ever to reinforce the St Petersburg Fortress. Only as late as June 1725 work was undertaken to rebuild the sixth and final Naryshkin Bastion. At this time the bastion was renamed, becoming the St Catherine Bastion, insofar as Russia was ruled already by Peter I's widow, the Empress Catherine I; still later the bastion was named the Empress Catherine Bastion. At the same time the Tsar Bastion also received a new name becoming the Peter I Bastion. The raising of stone walls was resumed only after Peter II replaced Catherine I on the throne in 1727. To oversee this process, the eminent statesman, military engineer Burehard Christoph von Münnich was appointed Head Director of Fortifications. When Peter II moved to Moscow in connection with his impending coronation, Münnich received "directorship" over St Petersburg and the entire St Petersburg Province. Under his leadership the construction of the Zotov Bastion was finished in 1728, and in 1729 the Peter II Bastion (formerly the Menshikov Bastion) was completed. In 1730 workers set out to finish the Golovkin Bastion, which had been renamed the "St Anne Bastion" (in honour of the saint after whom the new Empress Anna was named, succeeding Peter II to the throne in the same year); later the bastion was renamed the Empress Anna Bastion. During reconstruction of the fortress, the irregularly-shaped hexagon, whose corners were made up of the salient angles of the bastions, became somewhat wider at its east-west axis. In the reconstructed bastions the faces consisted of two brick walls, the space between which was filled with earth; by contrast the flanks consisted of two brick walls with casemates arranged on two floors between them.

In three of the six reconstructed curtain walls there appeared new fortress gates: The Vasilyevsky (Basil) Island Gate in the curtain wall between the Trubetskoi and Zotov Bastions (named the Vasilyevsky Island Curtain Wall), the Second Kronwerk Gate (later St Nicholas Gate) in the curtain wall between the Zotov Bastion and St Anne Bastion (named the St Nicholas Curtain Wall), and the First Kronwerk Gate (later the Kronwerk Gate) in the curtain wall between the St Anne and Peter II Bastions (named the Kronwerk Curtain Wall).

In 1731 reconstruction began of the ravelin covering the St Peter Curtain Wall, which was called the St John Ravelin (the name of the saint after whom the Empress Anna's father had been named). The gate in the left face of this ravelin was also rebuilt and renamed the St John Gate. Next to the ravelin two stone half-counterguards were erected, which were connected to the ravelin by traverses. The transversal moat, which had been dug back in 1703, was closed off at the ends near the salient angles of the Peter I Bastion and the Peter II Bastion by two batardeaus.

half-counterguard — a "П"-shaped exterior auxiliary fortress structure erected immediately before a leg (of a bastion or demi-bastion) to provide cover for it

traverse — a hollow wall connecting two auxiliary fortress structures

batardeau — exterior auxiliary fortress structure having the form of a stone dike with water gates, located in the fortress moat for regulating the water level in the moat; on the dike a small tower and a metal fence complete the system

In 1733 construction began of the St Alexei Ravelin (the Empress Anna's grandfather had been named after this saint). The stone ravelin, with gates in both faces, protected the Vasilyevsky Island Curtain Wall. Two stone half-counterguards were erected nearby and were linked with the ravelin by means of traverses.

Another ditch was dug across the island. It was covered at the salient angles of the Trubetskoi and Zotov Bastions by two more batardeaus. Much later, in 1800, a passage was cut in the batardeau at the salient angle of the Zotov Bastion.

The outside walls of the reconstructed fortress were whitewashed with lime mixed with dark red crushed brick.

In 1731 reconstruction began of the cavalier within the St Anne Bastion (the cavalier was encircled with ditches, which were filled in 1812), and a stone tower was built above the St Catherine Bastion with a flagstaff on top.

In 1738 reconstruction began of the bridge leading from the St John Ravelin to St Petersburg Island. The stone drawbridge with wooden central parts was named the St Peter Bridge.

ramp — a sloping ascent for the purpose of rolling guns from the inside of the fortress to the upper platform of one of its bastions

Axonometric drawing of the St Petersburg Fortress — detail of a page from an album of engravings entitled *Map of the Capital City of St Petersburg with Its Most Significant Views*, published by the Imperial Academy of Sciences and Arts in St Petersburg in 1753. The page which is shown in detail here, as well as the map of the city as a whole, are arranged so that their lower edge corresponds to the northern direction of the actual location (Library of the USSR Academy of Sciences, Leningrad)

Detail of a page from the album of engravings *Map of the Capital City of St Petersburg...* showing the St Petersburg Fortress (The Russian Museum, Leningrad)

→

Panorama of the St Petersburg Fortress from the Neva — a drawing dating to the late 18th century. In the St Alexei Ravelin (left) there is no triangular Secret House; to the west of the cathedral the large building of the Mint Works has not yet been built. Behind the fortress can be seen a portion of St Petersburg Island, whose buildings remind one of provincial Russian cities at the late 18th — early 19th centuries (Central Archives of the Film- , Phono- and Photo-documents, Leningrad)

Even before the reconstruction of the entire fortress was complete in 1740 (except for the kronwerk), the afore-mentioned Jacques Savary des Bruslons wrote in his *Dictionnaire universel de commerce* that, in the opinion of many, the St Petersburg Fortress is second to none in terms of its strength including the world-famous fortress of Dunkerque in northern France.

In 1748 the opening in the curtain wall between the Peter I and St Catherine Bastions was converted to a gate (this became the Neva Gate and the Neva Curtain Wall), and the Neva façade of the fortress was whitewashed with lime. In 1751 brick ramps were built, with casemates inside, leading up to the bastions.

In 1752 Abram Gannibal, a native African sent in his youth by Peter the Great to France to study engineering, was appointed Director of the Building Section of the Engineering Department in St Petersburg. Gannibal was the matriarchal great-grandfather of the

famous Russian poet Alexander Pushkin, who described the former in his short story *The Moor of Peter the Great*. Gannibal led work on various portions of the St Petersburg Fortress without making major structural changes. Under his direction reconstruction of the earthen kronwerk was begun to provide it a stone foundation. In 1756 the fortifications of the kronwerk were partially faced with brick, and in the period of 1760—74 they were reveted with stone slabs. As regards the fortification of the fortress proper (the structures located on Fortress Island itself), in 1756, according to Abram Gannibal's plan, portions of the walls were partially faced with stone slabs, and in 1760 plans were drawn up for the "dressing" of the fortress walls along the Neva River in granite. In 1764, at the decree of the Empress Catherine II, work began on facing the Admiralty side of St Petersburg bordering the Neva with granite slabs, since that part of the city had become central. In order to give the Neva façade of the St Petersburg Fortress a no less splendid look, in 1779, at the personal order of the Empress, work was begun to revet it in granite as well. In 1790, with the addition of eleven small towers at the corners on the walls along the Neva, the "dressing" of the fortress façade in granite was complete. This "dressing" served almost no defence purpose whatsoever.

By 1808, when the last Russian-Swedish war broke out, the St Petersburg Fortress was ready to repulse any enemy. However, the war ended rather quickly with the signing on September 5, 1809, in the Finnish city of Fredrikshamn (today Hamina) of a Russian-Swedish peace treaty which has been observed by both sides for almost 180 years now. This treaty was of major significance for Finland: with it Finland began its transformation from a Swedish colony into an independent nation.

←

Lithograph from the 1820s with a representation of the Neva pier, onto which is filing a procession of clergy following high mass in the cathedral (The Russian Museum, Leningrad)

During the War of 1812 the main force of the invading French army under the Emperor Napoleon I was directed at Moscow. However, preparations were made in the northern capital as well, and the St Petersburg Fortress was once again made battle-ready.

After a period of relative quiet in the late eighteenth and early nineteenth centuries, interest in the fortress as a strategic point was reawakened by the Emperor Nicholas I who ruled Russia from 1825 to 1855 and dabbled in the art of military engineering. In 1826 Nicholas I ordered that the fortress be classified as a first-class citadel, thus making it the main fortress in Russia. In 1827, according to plans approved by the Emperor, work was begun to update all the defensive structures located on Fortress Island. This work continued until 1840 and went on simultaneously with the rebuilding of the fortifications of Crohnstadt and its outlying forts. Thus, during the second quarter of the nineteenth century all the systems of permanent fortified structures in the eastern part of the Gulf of Finland were being updated.

Marking the completion of work on the modernization of the defensive structures of Fortress Island, as it were, in September 1840, large-scale war manoeuvres took place in St Petersburg, during which an imitation storming of the fortress from its northern side was successfully repelled.

Nevertheless, the condition of the kronwerk fortifications remained unsatisfactory throughout the 1830s. In 1849 Nicholas I approved a plan drawn up at his direction which provided the construction of a three-storey stone defence arsenal within the kronwerk, and the work was commenced in the next year. The battle might of this arsenal surpassed all of the fortress bastions, and it took on the defence functions of the Empress Anna

defence arsenal — an interior auxiliary fortress structure, serving for defence in time of siege, as well as for storage of arms and military equipment

Detail of a page from the album of lithographs entitled *Panorama of the City of St Petersburg* (the album was printed at the famous Paris typographer's Lemercier). The interior of the St Catherine Bastion looked like this during the second half of the 1840s and beginning of the 1850s (The Russian Museum, Leningrad)

Bastion. Subsequently, in 1852, the Emperor confirmed a plan for rebuilding and reinforcing the old fortifications of the kronwerk.

In the autumn of 1853 war between Russia and Turkey broke out, and England and France soon joined in against Russia (this war, which ended in 1856, was called the Crimean War, since the main military theatre was the Crimea Peninsula). And thus once again the St Petersburg Fortress went on battle alert, but didn't have the opportunity to fire at its opponents since the approach to the Neva delta by English and French vessels entering the Gulf of Finland was deterred by Russian mines.

In 1855 Nicholas I died. His successor, Alexander II, was much less keen on the fortress as a military object, and in 1856 it was decided not to carry out most of the work that had been provided for under the plan signed in 1852. Some of the stone from the old dilapidated kronwerk fortifications was hauled away and within the period of 1874—77, in the interest of freeing space for artillery warehouses, the eighteenth-century fortifications were almost completely destroyed. The only remaining trace is a significant depression and raised area corresponding to the rampart which had once stood there. With regard to the glacis which surrounded the kronwerk on the east, north and west, it is worth mentioning that the Ministry of Finance, which dealt with this part of St Petersburg Island during the reign of Nicholas I, desiring to somehow improve its appearance, began in 1842 to lay out a park on the glacis, naming it the Alexander Park in honour of Nicholas I's brother, Alexander I (today the Lenin Park).

In 1865 a zoological park opened in the western part of the former glacis (now the Leningrad Zoo). In 1900 in the Alexander Park the Folk House was opened (subsequently this building was added onto many times, reconstructed, and changed owners). In 1906 the Orthopedic Institute (today the Vreden Institute of Traumatology and Orthopedics) was opened in the park and in 1911 a monument dedicated to the sailors of the destroyer *Steregushchy*, which was sunk during the Russo-Japanese War of 1904—5, was installed.

Back on Fortress Island in the mid-nineteenth century the gates in the St Alexei Ravelin were closed up, and in 1874 the St Nicholas Gate was widened, and both façades were redone. During the period beginning in the mid-nineteenth century and including the beginning of the twentieth century, almost all the curtain walls were rebuilt from two-storey into one-storey structures. In 1880—82 the canal traversing the island was filled in with building refuse. In 1889—92 the moat in front of the St Peter Curtain Wall was filled in, and in 1893 the same was done with the

→

Portion of the engraving *Overall View of St Petersburg and Its Environs* printed in Paris, providing a bird's-eye-view of the city as it looked at the beginning of the 1860s, with the St Petersburg Fortress in the centre (Y. M. Denisov collection)

At the St Peter Gate in May 1902 awaiting the arrival at the fortress of the French President Emile Loubet. The St Peter Curtain Wall has not yet been rebuilt from a two-storey into a one-storey structure (Central Archives of the Film-, Phono- and Photo-documents, Leningrad)

Officer and junior officer with a group of soldiers at the batardeau of the Trubetskoi Bastion. The grate of the batardeau is hidden by a brick wall. In the background, the St Catherine Bastion with its guns and flagstaff tower, and farther back the permanent Trinity Bridge. Early 20th century (Central Archives of the Film-, Phono- and Photo-documents, Leningrad)

moat in front of the Vasilyevsky Island Curtain Wall.

In 1892 work commenced on the construction of a permanent bridge (the Trinity, today Kirov Bridge) extending from the left bank of the Neva to St Petersburg Island. The floating bridge which had earlier joined the two river banks at this point was temporarily moved downstream during the construction period and installed so that it would lead to the fortress itself. In order to provide a thoroughfare through the fortress the grates were removed from the batardeaus near the Peter I and Peter II Bastions, a roadbed was laid over the filled-in moat in front of the St Peter Curtain Wall, and across the Kronwerk Strait another temporary wooden bridge was built.

After the beginning of World War I in 1914, and in connection with the official renaming of St Petersburg to Petrograd, the fortress as well came to be called the Petrograd Fortress. As the battle-field was distant from the northern Russian capital, the role that the fortress played was limited to receiving a few groups of war prisoners.

So the military history of the St Petersburg Fortress in pre-revolutionary Russia was quite unusual. The fortress on more than one occasion prepared for battle, it was rebuilt, armed, reinforced, but the enemy never once got close enough to be within its firing range. Throughout its pre-revolutionary history the St Petersburg Fortress never was exclusively a military object.

Early on the fortress became one of the main centres of the celebration of Russian military victories. As already mentioned, the first salute from the fortress walls rang out in 1704 in honour of the victory on Lake Peipus, and this tradition continues even today. In 1710, during the celebration of the taking of Vyborg, captured Swedish banners were carried into the wooden fortress cathedral, and this ceremony marked the beginning of the collection in the Sts Peter and Paul Cathedral of relics of Russian military valour.

For a long time the fortress housed the boat, which was built in England in the seventeenth century and presented to Peter I's father, Tsar Alexei Mikhailovich, and which became in 1688 the first vessel in which the young Peter studied navigation by sailing the River Yauza in the environs of Moscow and Lake Pleshcheyevo near Pereslavl-Zalessky. In the spring of 1723 the boat was transferred to St Petersburg, where it was festively welcomed by "the sounds of music, cymbals, horns and a whole assortment of other instruments and with cannon fire", and mounted on a pedestal on which, among other things, was written "Child's play has brought manhood's courageous triumph." At the end of the summer the small vessel, the "Grandfather" of the Russian Navy, was solemnly accompanied by the thunderous sound of a military salute as it led the Russian fleet out to the Gulf of Finland, after which it was turned over to the Commandant of the St Petersburg Fortress for preservation. On several occasions to follow the boat was made a "participant" in various ceremonies. One such occasion took place in 1724 when the relics of the patron saint of St Petersburg — the Grand Prince Alexander Nevsky — were brought from Vladimir to St Petersburg, and again in 1803 during the celebration of the

Lithograph representing the ceremonial crossing of the Neva on April 20, 1858, marking the seasonal thaw of the river (and annual opening of the port) published in *Russian Art Bulletin* of the same year. The upper part of the cathedral bell-tower and the drum and cupola above the eastern part of the cathedral are covered with scaffolding — the wooden structures of the bell-tower and small cupola above the dome are being replaced with metal ones (The Russian Museum, Leningrad)

centennial of the founding of the city on the Neva.

On November 8, 1889, in the Defense Arsenal located in the kronwerk, the 500-year anniversary of Russian artillery was celebrated.

Of no less interest were several "non-military" observances which took place in the fortress. Thus, each spring, beginning in the second half of the eighteenth century, the thawing of the Neva and opening of the navigation season were celebrated in special way. The main figure in this celebration was the Director of the City Shipyard, built in 1781 on the right bank of the river just below the top of the delta for the construction and repair of merchant vessels. After three cannon shots from the St Petersburg Fortress the Director of the Shipyard sailed out to the fortress at the head of a whole flotilla of sailboats, saluted the fortress with seven cannon shots, and after a reply salute, turned and headed for the opposite bank to the Winter Palace and saluted the main residence of the Emperor. Following 1831 the ceremonial crossing of the Neva to salute the Winter Palace was headed by the Commandant of the fortress.

However, the "non-military" role of the fortress was not limited to such festivities. From 1711 to 1714 the fortress housed the Senate,

at that time the highest collegiate directive organ in the country, established "in place of His Majesty, the Tsar's own person".
In 1719 it was decided to transfer from Moscow to St Petersburg the production of money. Thus, the Mint Works was opened in the St Petersburg Fortress in 1724. Up until the October Revolution of 1917 it remained the main centre for minting Russian coins, closing its doors only for the temporary periods of 1728—38 (in connection with the move of the Imperial court to Moscow) and 1799—1805 (in connection with the construction of a new building for the mint and its re-equipment). In 1876 the St Petersburg Mint Works became the sole mint in Russia.
The Mint Works became the site in 1829 of the "collection of samples of foreign weights and measures". This greatly aided the work which was carried out in the 1830s to standardize weights and measures in Russia.
Under different titles from 1796 to 1860 the fortress housed the main organization charged with holding government funds in pre-revolutionary Russia, the Treasury Department.
As in many Western European cities at the beginning of the eighteenth century, windmills stood on the fortress bastions. At the end of the 1710s the fortress casemates were rented out to St Petersburg merchants as warehouse space. At this time the main apothecary was also located in the fortress.
Even in the first years of the fortress construction and repair of various vessels took place on the site of the future kronwerk. In 1805 the kronwerk was almost completely taken over by the City Shipyard. In 1808 a shipbuilding school was established at the kronwerk shipyard.
In 1838—40 the fortress housed one of the first electro-technical workshops in the world.
From 1731 to 1858 the Sts Peter and Paul Cathedral was officially the main city cathedral,

and thus one of two main centres of religious life in St Petersburg (the second centre being the St Alexander Nevsky Monastery located upstream on the Neva). When in 1858 St Isaac's Cathedral officially replaced the Sts Peter and Paul Cathedral as the main centre for worship, the latter became the cathedral of the Tsar's family and the court.

Up until the beginning of the eighteenth century the burial vault of the Romanov dynasty (ruling from 1613) remained the Archangel Michael Cathedral in the Moscow Kremlin, where in even earlier times all the Grand Princes of Moscow and Vladimir, beginning with Ioann I Danilovich (the Kalita) and all the tsars descending from the line of Rurik were buried. In 1708 the wooden Sts Peter and Paul Cathedral was made the second burial vault of the Romanov family. And in 1725 it was made the main burial vault of the Romanovs' when, after Peter I's death, the coffin with his body was placed on a special base in the as yet unfinished church. (The coffin was interred in the cathedral in 1731). In the beginning of the twentieth century members of the Romanov family were likewise buried in the Grand Ducal Burial Vault built specially for this purpose in the fortress next to the cathedral.

Beginning in 1873 cannon shots were fired daily from the fortress informing St Petersburg citizens of the approach of midday (12:00 noon). Shots were also fired from the fortress to warn of flood danger.

From the very beginning of its existence, the fortress maintained for more than 200 years, besides the above-mentioned functions, yet another one, that of a prison.
A study of the fortress prison records shows that major criminals were kept here on several occasions. For example, in 1715 the main criminal investigation office, located in the fortress, led the investigation of a group of bribe-takers and embezzlers of state property, the head of which turned out to be the St Petersburg Vice-Governor Yakov Korsakov. The fortress also served more than once as a military prison. In 1820 soldiers from the Semionovsky Regiment were imprisoned here. They had protested the inhuman treatment of their regimental commander, and after that still other soldiers arrived from the same regiment who had stood up for their arrested comrades. Beginning in the 1910s the fortress was used almost exclusively as a military prison. In 1916 the Minister of War, Vladimir Sukhomlinov, was accused of treason and held here. But, for the most part, in pre-revolutionary times the fortress served as a political prison. As early as 1721 the Holstein nobleman Friedrich Wilhelm Berkholz, author of a most interesting diary containing valuable information about the St Petersburg of Peter I's time, upon seeing the St Petersburg Fortress, was reminded of the Paris Bastille, which from the mid-seventeenth century was used exclusively as a prison for political opponents of the kings. Berkholz knew well that in the St Petersburg Fortress "all state criminals are held and often tortures are carried out in secret."
In 1718 the fortress was the centre for the investigation of the adherents of Peter's son, Prince Alexei, who had long been in conflict with his father. Deprived by Peter of all rights to the Russian throne, in the summer of the same year Alexei was thrown into

the prison built in the Trubetskoi Bastion, and died there.
In 1740, in the Secret Police Office located in the fortress, the interrogation and torture of a group of people took place who had aspired to weaken the influence on the Empress Anna of her close associates of foreign descent, in particular her long-time favourite, Ernst Johann von Biron. The head of this group was the Cabinet Minister Alexei Volynsky. Volynsky, together with two of his adherents, was beheaded at the Sytny Market not far from the kronwerk in the summer of 1740. In the same year the Empress Anna died, and Ioann Antonovich, the two-month-old son of the Empress' niece, Anna Leopoldovna, was proclaimed the new Emperor. Biron was appointed regent until Ioann Antonovich would come of age. Inasmuch as Biron repeatedly humiliated the child-ruler's mother, not even one month had passed before Burehard Christoph von Münnich (mentioned earlier in connection with the construction of stone walls of the fortress) had arrested Biron, and Anna Leopoldovna had become the ruler of the state. However, in the following year of 1741, Anna Leopoldovna lost power as the result of a coup carried out by the guard in favour of Peter I's daughter Elizabeth, who became the new Russian Empress. Now the fortress prison became home for the noblemen who had supported the former ruler, and among them was Münnich.

One of the Empress Elizabeth's closest people was her personal surgeon Johann-Hermann Lestocq, who took an active role in preparing the coup of 1741. Nevertheless, in 1748 Lestocq was accused of treason, arrested, and held in the St Petersburg Fortress until 1753.
In 1790 the head of St Petersburg Customs, Alexander Radishchev, was put in the fortress prison for writing and publishing a book in protest of serfdom, *A Journey from St*

Petersburg to Moscow. He was sentenced to ten years of exile in Siberia. The Empress Catherine II led the investigation personally in the matter of the author and publisher of *A Journey*, even though she, in the beginning of her reign, had demonstrated the intent of acting on humane principles in regard to her fellow countrymen when she had recommended sending a group of students abroad, among them Alexander Radishchev, to study "Natural and Social Law".

On December 14, 1825, the first anti-governmental army uprising in Russian history took place in St Petersburg. Its leaders were intent on abolishing the Tsar's autocracy. From this day on the history of the revolutionary movement in Russia began, a movement which reached its culmination with the victory of the October Socialist Revolution in 1917. And from this day on, the St Petersburg Fortress became the place where the most determined and most consistent opponents of the Tsarist regime were imprisoned. Besides the casemates in the fortress walls, another two special prison buildings were used for this purpose built in the Alexei Ravelin and in the Trubetskoi Bastion.

Until well into the year 1826 the fortress was the place of mass detainment of participants of the brutally crushed uprising of December 14. Five of the leaders were hung (on the kronwerk rampart). In 1849 the fortress became a prison for participants of the regular meetings ("Fridays") which had taken place starting in 1845 at the home of the translator of the Ministry of Foreign Affairs, Mikhail Butashevich-Petrashevsky (they are also known as the Petrashevsky Circle). The members of the circle were arrested for their criticism at these meetings of the present Russian political regime. Beginning in the 1860s members of different secret revolutionary organizations were held in the fortress — "Earth and Will" (in 1863), "The Organization" and "Hell" (in 1866), and "The People's Will" (in 1881). "The People's Will", formed in 1879, was the main Russian revolutionary organization created by the *raznochintsy*, intellectuals not belonging to the gentry. The group's main task was the political battle against autocracy; its main ideas were the calling of a constituent assembly, instituting of general voting rights, providing in Russia for the freedoms of speech, conscience, press and assembly. However, to achieve its goals "The People's Will" chose the erroneous methods of terror. The culmination of the terrorist activities of the group was the assasination in St Petersburg of the Emperor Alexander II on March 1, 1881, after which began the routing of the organization by the government. In 1887 members of the "Terrorist faction of 'The People's Will' party" were arrested in preparation to assassinate the Emperor Alexander III and brought to the fortress. Following their trial, five of the members, including the creator of the faction's platform, Alexander Ulyanov, the older brother of Vladimir Ulyanov (Lenin), were executed in Schlüsselburg. Lenin thus evaluated the activities of the group: "They doubtlessly contributed — directly or indirectly — to the subsequent revolutionary education of the Russian people. But they did not, and could not, achieve their immediate aim of generating a people's revolution."

In 1896—97 there were more arrests: members of the group organized in 1895 in St Petersburg by Lenin known as the Union of the Struggle for the Freeing of the Working Class, the first proletarian Marxist revolutionary organization in Russia and direct forerunner of the Russian Social-Democratic Workers' Party (RSDWP). And from 1898 to 1904 major activists of the RSDWP were confined in the fortress, along with those united around the

first Russian Marxist newspaper *Iskra* (*Spark*) founded by Lenin, which was printed illegally in Munich, London and Geneva, and was illegally distributed in Russia.

After the event which became the direct impetus for the First Russian Revolution, i.e., the shooting of a peaceful workers' demonstration in front of the Winter Palace (the Tsar's main residence) on January 9, 1905, the fortress prison was overrun with protesters of this bloody act of the Tsar.

"Years passed one after the other," wrote P. Polivanov, one of the fortress prisoners, a member of "The People's Will" group, "whole generations have changed, the thoughts and feelings which influenced society have changed, the victims have changed, the executioners have changed; but the Peter and Paul Fortress remains unchanged, ever gloomy, ever ominous, ever willing to take into its casemates victims of tyranny and ignorance. What a terrible picture it would be if it were possible to collect into one all of the horrors which were committed in this Russian Bastille since the first days of its existence!.. So many grand plans, so many broken hopes, so many bright ideas and feelings have been buried within the walls of the various bastions, curtain walls, and ravelins of this fortress."

Indeed, among the prisoners in the fortress not a few ended their days here; among them were those who lost their minds; there were also those whom fear drove to betrayal and desertion. But the majority of the political prisoners stubbornly withstood all of the horrors of solitary confinement, all of the torments by their investigators and prison guards, and when set free, continued their struggle against the monarchy.

History of the fortress

The St Petersburg (Peter and Paul) Fortress went down in the history of the Russian revolutionary movement not only as a prison, but also as a primary military object, always figuring in the strategies of both revolutionaries and their opponents.

On December 14, 1825, only a few hours following the armed anti-governmental uprising, the Emperor Nicholas I ordered that the fortress gates be locked and that the guns be loaded with buck-shot. In case of the further spreading of the uprising, the fortress was to become the main support centre for the government forces. And for that matter certain leaders of the uprising also considered use of the fortress in the struggle against the government.

In the beginning of the 1880s members of "The People's Will" planned armed revolutionary action in St Petersburg and one of their primary operations was to be the seizing of the St Petersburg Fortress.

In the years of the First Russian Revolution of 1905—7 the fortress was one of the main centres of the autocracy in its struggle with democratic forces. In 1906 the St Petersburg Military Tribunal was established in the fortress, one of the most cruel punitive institutions of Tsarism ever seen for the purpose of reprisal against those who sought the liquidation of the monarchy in Russia. Each of these courts was comprised of five regular officers and intentionally no one with a background in law was allowed to attend; neither the prosecuting side, nor the defence were professionally represented; the sentences were to be handed down no later than two days after their initial consideration by the court, and took effect immediately; no recourse being allowed, sentences were carried out within twenty-four hours.

But during the second (February) and third (October) revolutions, the role of the fortress was completely different.

On February 27, 1917, the soldiers of the Fourth Company of the Pavlovsky Regiment who came out on the side of the rebelling workers were imprisoned. But already in the morning of February 28 the fortress and its armed bastions surrendered without a single shot to the Military Commission of the Petrograd Soviet of Workers' Deputies. The bloodless seizure of the fortress predetermined the surrender to the rebels on the same day of the Admiralty Building — the last stronghold of the old regime in Petrograd. The fortress began to fill with arrested Tsarist ministers and other high officials. Their illegal activities while in office were investigated by a Special Investigating Commission which was convened within the prison in the Trubetskoi Bastion. The well-known Russian poet, playwright and critic, Alexander Blok, was a member of this commission.

On October 20, 1917, in the Smolny Institute Building (the building had since August housed the All-Russian Central Executive Committee of the Soviets of Workers' and Soldiers' Deputies), a special body of the Petrograd Soviet, the Petrograd Military-Revolutionary Committee, began its activities. The committee was created for the preparation and execution of an armed uprising against the Provisional Government for the purpose of establishing Soviet power in the recently (September 1) declared Russian Republic. On October 23, the committee took control over the Peter and Paul Fortress together with its arsenal, where over 100,000 rifles were stored. On October 24, it was decided to make the fortress the field headquarters of the revolution.

According to the plans of the Petrograd Military-Revolutionary Committee, the uprising was to be culminated by a storm of the Winter Palace, the seat of the Provisional Government. It was decided that the signal to start the storm would be a shot from the Catherine (Naryshkin) Bastion.

At approximately seven o'clock in the evening of October 25 the field headquarters of the revolution sent an ultimatum to the Headquarters of the Petrograd Military District located next to the Winter Palace which read: "The guns of the Peter and Paul Fortress and the ships *Aurora*, *Amur* and others are aimed at the Winter Palace and the building of the Main Headquarters. In the name of the Military-Revolutionary Committee we demand the capitulation of the members of the Provisional Government and of the military forces subordinate to it." After the refusal of the Provisional Government to accept this ultimatum, at nine o'clock in the evening the signal was given from the fortress and, after the firing of a blank shot from the bow guns of the cruiser *Aurora*, the storming of the Winter Palace commenced.

Around 2 a.m. in the morning of October 26, the ministers arrested in the palace were brought to the fortress. Meanwhile, at the Smolny, delegates of the Second All-Russian Congress of the Soviets of Workers' and Soldiers' Deputies ratified the appeal which read: "On the basis of the will of the vast majority of workers, soldiers and peasants, on the basis of the victorious uprising of workers and military forces of the garrison in Petrograd, the Congress now takes power into its hands."

Soon after the victory of the October Socialist Revolution, organs of Soviet power began to implement special measures for the preservation of the Peter and Paul Fortress as a historical and architectural complex. Prior to the Revolution the Sts Peter and Paul Cathedral was considered the main attraction on Fortress Island. In the summer of 1917 the cathedral suffered the fate of many other Petrograd museums and historical buildings: by order of the Provisional Government, considering the threat of approaching German forces, all of the items hand-made by Peter I, together with manuscripts and books published in Russia before the eighteenth century, the most valuable icons and ecclesiastical vestments were evacuated from the cathedral and transferred to Moscow. The Provisional Government delegated the preservation of the cathedral itself, as well as the Grand Ducal Burial Vault and the house in which Peter the Great's boat was kept, to the cathedral's resident clergy.

View of the fortress from the Palace Embankment in 1921. Townspeople salvage firewood from a wooden barge dragged up on the embankment. A page from the album of engravings *Petersburg: Ruins and Revival*, published in Petrograd in 1923 (The Russian Museum, Leningrad)

The Peter and Paul Fortress. A page from the album of lithographs *Petersburg in '21*, published by the Committee for the Popularization of Art Publications of the Russian Academy of the History of Material Culture in Petrograd in 1923 (The Russian Museum, Leningrad)

Less than two years after the Revolution organs of Soviet power took on the preservation of these buildings. On May 27, 1919, when the spring campaign was launched against Petrograd by the White Army, the buildings were examined and sealed by a special state commission. Its members insisted that a protective zone be created around the entire fortress. Emphasizing in their report that the Peter and Paul Fortress represents "a monument of great historical and cultural value", they further stated: "The silhouette of the cathedral together with the fortress constitutes the main and most characteristic landmark of the Petrograd skyline, without which the city would not be quite the same. Therefore, it is of the utmost importance that in the future this silhouette be preserved, and in so doing attention should be given to all those structures erected or reconstructed inside the fortress as weľl as those nearby, for any change will disrupt that wonderful harmony which is created by the horizontal lines of the fortress and the sharp vertical lines of the cathedral's spire." The members of the commission insisted on immediately placing the cathedral and Boathouse under special legal protective status.

On September 24, 1919, because of the autumn campaign launched on Petrograd by the White Army, military authorities were required to take the entire Peter and Paul Fortress under their control, making it the centre of the city's internal defence. Nevertheless, city officials continued to emphasize the necessity of the preservation of the historical structures on Fortress Island. In spite of the extremely short supply of firewood in Petrograd (practically the only available source of heat in the city) during the Civil War, provisions were made for the regular heating of the cathedral so that this outstanding architectural monument would be safe from dampness.

The St John Gate, decorated for the celebration of the second anniversary of the October Revolution. The board on the left bears the name of the main body of direction of military personnel (located in the fortress) protecting the city in the autumn of 1919 — "The Headquarters of Internal Defence of the City of Petrograd"; the board on the right bears a representation of a naval fortress above which furls a flag with the same title mentioned above. On its walls is written: "Gibraltar of the Revolution" (Central Archives of the Film-, Phono- and Photo-documents, Leningrad)

The Sts Peter and Paul Cathedral attracted popular interest from the very start of Soviet power. As early as 1918 the question of organizing tours of Fortress Island was being discussed. However, it was impossible to grant broad access to visitors to view its historical and cultural sights until December 3, 1920, the end of the Civil War and the date when the state of siege was officially lifted in Petrograd. Thereafter, in July 1920, the first excursion group made an official tour of the fortress, a group consisting of delegates of the Second Congress of the Third International. Tours of the fortress commenced on a regular basis beginning in the summer of 1922.

The end of the war allowed more effective measures to be taken for the preservation of the whole fortress as a complex of architectural and historical monuments. The Trubetskoi Bastion and the prison facilities within it, closely tied to the history of the Russian revolutionary movement, became one of the main attractions of the fortress. In 1923, by order of the highest military authorities, the

The Neva bank of Fortress Island during improvement work begun in 1925 and completed for the 10th Anniversary of the October Revolution. The grate of the batardeau of the Trubetskoi Bastion is still hidden by a brick wall (Central Archives of the Film-, Phono- and Photodocuments, Leningrad)

bastion and prison were made part of the Museum of the Revolution. In the same year allocations were made for the first restoration work to be carried out during Soviet times on the Sts Peter and Paul Cathedral, and a custodian-architect was assigned to maintain it. In 1924 specialists began work on restoration of the cathedral interior, keeping in mind that the cathedral is not only an architectural landmark, but a historical monument as well. However, restoration of just the cathedral and prison facilities in the Trubetskoi Bastion was not enough to make the entire fortress accessible to the inhabitants and visitors of Leningrad. Therefore, in the period from 1925 to 1927 large-scale improvements were made on Fortress Island: roads and lawns were layed out; new bushes and trees were planted, and its banks were reinforced. The decision was made at this time to restore the grate of the batardeau on the eastern end of the island, which had been removed in 1892.

True, the major part of the fortress still remained under the command of the military —

A decorative composition in the style of Constructivism erected at the salient angle of the Naryshkin Bastion in 1930 on the occasion of the 25th Anniversary of the First Russian Revolution. Battle guns are still in place on the bastion (Central Archives of the Film-, Phono- and Photo-documents, Leningrad)

in the first decades following the Revolution Leningrad was essentially a border city. However, both military and municipal authorities understood that in the future the entire fortress should become an object of special care and use, namely as a museum-citadel. The only remaining building of a non-museum nature that was to remain was the Mint Works (it had been partially dismantled in 1918, but already in 1921 had resumed production). During the 1920s and 1930s much was done for the preservation of the Peter and Paul Fortress by the volunteer scientific society "Old Petersburg — New Leningrad", among whose main tasks it was to facilitate the best use of historical and architectural monuments of St Petersburg under the new conditions of the socialist reconstruction of Leningrad.

During the siege of Leningrad by Nazi forces, lasting from September 8, 1941, to January 27, 1944, everything possible was done in order to save the historical and architectural monuments of the fortress, which were once again under command of Soviet military authorities. The gilt spire of the Sts Peter and Paul Cathedral was camouflaged. In December 1942 soldiers of the local air defence force completed work to protect the cathedral from the destructive effects of dampness, repairing the roof which had been damaged by shell fragments and sealing the windows, in which almost no glass remained.

Today on the grounds of the almost completely restored fortress new exhibitions appear one after another, created by the State Museum of the History of Leningrad, and different folk festivals take place from time to time. The entire fortress is now accessible for viewing.

The fortress today

A tour of the fortress is best begun on Petrograd Island, from the intersection of Kirov Prospekt and Kuibyshev Street. The streets are named in honour of Sergei Kirov (1886—1934), the leader of the Leningrad party organization in 1926—34, and Valerian Kuibyshev (1888—1935), an eminent Soviet political and military figure, respectively. This intersection forms one of the corners of Revolution Square (formerly Trinity Square, the oldest square in the city). A few dozen steps away, connecting Petrograd and Hare Islands, a wide wooden bridge spans across the Kronwerk Strait, which since the end of the nineteenth century has been called the St John Bridge. In the past nearly everyone to enter the fortress — from members of the Emperor's family and high-ranking foreigners participating in various formal ceremonies in the cathedral to convicts held at the fortress prison — everyone passed over this bridge. Construction of the bridge began in 1738 and was completed by 1740. In the course of restoration work in 1953, street lamps were installed on the bridge, which are exact copies of those which adorned the entrances to the pontoon bridge which, until 1892, connected the left bank of the Neva with St Petersburg (now Petrograd) Island. The posts of some of the lamps are in the form of a bundle of lances with garlands and two-headed eagles at the top; others are mounted on obelisks crowned with military helmets; all the posts are likewise adorned with representations of oval shields on crossed swords. In addition, in 1953 the wrought-iron railing was restored on the St John Bridge, with posts in the shape of lictor fasces, a bundle of rods having among them an ax with the blade projecting borne before Roman magistrates in ancient times as an insignia of authority.

From the St John Bridge the brick half-counterguard of the Menshikov Bastion is

The St John Bridge, Ravelin and Gate

socle — the bottommost protruding portion of the wall of a building or structure located directly above the ground

cornice — a decorative detail of the façade of a building or structure or of one of its separate parts having the form of a horizontal or sloping decorative band

rusticated masonry — a decorative detail which creates the illusion of large stone blocks

pediment — a low-pitched gable above a portico in a façade of a building or structure framed on all sides by mouldings; it has a variety of forms — triangular or curved segmentally ("bow"-shaped), etc.; always set off or framed on all sides by mouldings and the upper member of the entablature

tympanum — the triangular recessed face of a pediment, framed on all sides by its mouldings

cartouche — a decorative detail in the form of a small shield with rolled-up edges on which monograms and coats-of-arms are often displayed

readily visible. The socle, cornice and corners of this fortification are reveted with limestone tiles. This is the way the exterior of the fortress walls looked after renovation in 1827—40.

A little farther along the right bank of the Kronwerk Strait is the huge brick building of the Defence Arsenal, the construction of which was completed in 1860.

The St John Bridge leads to the rather low St John Gate pierced in the left face of the St John Ravelin. The façade of the gate, decorated with rusticated masonry, is crowned with a triangular pediment, the tympanum of which encloses a cartouche and the image of the Russian Imperial crown surrounded by various military attributes and insignia — ban-

ners, halberds and drums. The date on the gate — the year 1740 — marks the completion of all stone defence structures of Fortress Island. The St John Gate is the place where one first sees a motif characteristic of and repeated in various other structures throughout the fortress, namely two pairs of pilasters. It is comparable with another motif which is also repeated in several places in the fortress, i.e., two pairs of columns. The architectural forms of the St John Gate are simple and resemble Renaissance architecture.

pilaster — decorative detail of a building or structure in the form of a vertical protrusion from the wall, usually decorated with a base at the bottom and a capital at the top

The fortress today

Passing through the St John Gate into the ravelin of the same name, one's attention is immediately drawn to the main gate of the fortress located in the centre of the curtain wall connecting the Tsar Bastion (on the left) and the Menshikov Bastion (on the right). Originally the main gate was crowned by a statue of St Peter; therefore, the gate itself, as well as the entire curtain wall in which it is located, have the same name — St Peter.

The St Peter Gate was constructed in 1717—18 replacing the original wooden main gate. Its appearance as a whole reminds one of Western European triumphal gates in the Baroque style as well as the main façades

The St John Gate

of Western European Baroque churches. The lower portion of the St Peter Gate is decorated with pilasters and rusticated masonry. Over a large arched opening is fixed a sculpture of the black two-headed eagle. On either side of the arch are statues of two women in niches (the one on the right clad in military attire; the one on the left wearing a long robe is holding a mirror and snake). Above this lower portion of the gate stretches an entablature, above which rises a richly decorated attic, consisting of a large rectangular wooden bas-relief bordered on either side by rusticated pilasters and volutes with smaller bas-reliefs, and topped by a curved pediment containing yet another bas-relief.

entablature — a complex horizontal element of decorative design located in the upper part of a façade or interior of a building or structure

attic — a decorative side wall having the appearance of a pedestal and located above the entablature which is intended for low-reliefs or wall paintings, etc.

volute — decorative detail in the form of a scroll

guardhouse — building used for housing the fortress guard, also for the detainment of arrested officers

The bas-relief in the tympanum portrays Sabaoth encircled by angels, and the two bas-reliefs near the volutes depict various military attributes. The large rectangular bas-relief is a complex multi-figured composition. In the centre, on a cliff, stands a fortress; above it, amidst swirling clouds, winged demons are flying. A bearded man with wings is falling out of the clouds right down onto the fortress. Below to the right and left people are standing, some of them pointing at the falling figure. Near the fortress on one side a beardless man in the dress of a Roman military leader stretches his hand out towards the structure: on the other side a woman is kneeling before the fortress.

In the beginning of the eighteenth century the citizens of St Petersburg, undoubtedly, perceived this large bas-relief as an integral component of the entire gate decoration, including likewise the image in the tympanum of the pediment and the statue of St Peter, which crowned the gate at that time. To help explain the meaning behind the entire composition it is interesting to compare it with another extremely curious monument of Russian culture of that time.

→

The St Peter Gate

In 1716 the St Petersburg Printing House issued a huge engraving, a panorama depicting the new Russian city on the Neva. In almost the very middle of the panorama the fortress is depicted with its main decoration at that time, the St Peter Gate. This engraving was presented in 1717 to Peter I, with a special explanatory text attached at the bottom, which was later titled *Descriptive Laud of the City of St Petersburg and Especially of Peter the Great, the Creator of This City.* The *Descriptive Laud* was compiled by the clergyman monk Gabriel Buzhinsky, an eminent writer of the epoch of Peter the Great, who, in particular, translated into Russian a great number of essays by Samuel Pufendorf, a noted seventeenth-century German Enlightener. The descriptive explanatory text compiled by Buzhinsky was given such great attention in the eighteenth century that Andrei Bogdanov, author of the first Russian description of St Petersburg, considered it essential to comment at length on the *Descriptive Laud* and to include it as a part of his book.

As the *Descriptive Laud* reads, the fortress was put under the protection of Sabaoth and St Peter, and was founded "on the hard rock of piety" and "named St Petersburg". The *Descriptive Laud* goes on to say that St Petersburg itself is also a rock, with which St Peter will strike all who attempt to encroach on the fortress, and that the "haughty Simon", infuriating the great protector of the fortress, St Peter, "shall fall and be broken on the rock"; it reads further that St Petersburg has yet another "great protector" — St Alexander Nevsky (the canonized Russian prince, under whose command on July 15, 1240, the Novgorodians were victorious over the Swedes on the Neva). If one recalls that the Greek word *petros* has cognates in the form of the masculine name Piotr (Russian), Pieter (Dutch), and Peter (German and English),

САНКТЪ ПИТЕРЪ БѸР

ST: PETERSBURGH

←

Portion of the engraving *St Petersburg*, issued in 1716 by the St Petersburg Printing House. It was supposed at that time that the fortress and the cathedral would look in the future as they are represented here

Left statue of the St Peter Gate

as well as a second meaning as a noun signifying a "rock" or "cliff", then it becomes obvious why Buzhinsky in his *Descriptive Laud* continually associates "rock" with the names "Peter" and "St Petersburg".

The idea automatically comes to mind of the close association of the image on the St Peter Gate with the basic ideas of the *Descriptive Laud.* Taking everything into account, one can conclude that Sabaoth is depicted in the tympanum as the protector of St Petersburg, which is portrayed in the centre of the bas-relief standing on a cliff. The bearded man with wings is undoubtedly the heathen sorcerer Simon Magus, who, according to the ancient Christian legend, at first defamed St Peter and then, with the support of demons, in order to prove his superiority, attempted to fly; however, St Peter drove the demons away with a prayer and Simon fell to the ground in disgrace. The beardless man in the garb of an ancient Roman officer is, more likely than not, Peter the Great, although it is also possible that this is St Alexander Nevsky. The kneeling woman appears from all indications to be a symbol of piety.

Thus, contrary to previous suppositions, the sculptural bas-relief composition, decorating the St Peter Gate since 1717—18, is not a symbolic portrayal of the victory of the Russians over Sweden, but rather was designed as a "laud" of the new Russian city by means of visual arts, as a symbol of its invincibility.

The sculptural image above the gate of the black two-headed eagle is cast in lead and weighs more than a ton. On the eagle's two heads are the Imperial crowns; in his talons a sceptre and orb; on his chest the red shield with a coat-of-arms depicting a rider on a white horse struggling with a winged dragon. This is the Russian Imperial coat-of-arms (the so-called State Eagle); the shield with the image of a rider (St George) striking a

The "State Eagle" above the St Peter Gate

Right statue of the St Peter Gate

dragon is the ancient coat-of-arms of Moscow. The Russian Imperial coat-of-arms acquired its present appearance in the second half of the nineteenth century, as here the rider in the Moscow coat-of-arms is turned to the heraldic right side (for the viewer to the left side). This turn was introduced only in 1856; before that the rider always faced left.

The statues which originally stood in the niches have not survived, and when the present ones were installed is also unknown. Opinions vary as to whom these statues portray. There is one supposition that the statue of the woman in military garb represents Athena Pallas or Bellona, while the statue of the woman with the mirror and snake represents — Truth, Poliade or Minerva.

It is believed that the architect who designed the St Peter Gate (the present stone gate as well as the previous wooden one) was Trezzini, that the large rectangular bas-relief was executed by the sculptor Hans Konrad Ossner, and that the small bas-reliefs on the volutes were done by the sculptor Nicolas Pineau. The rectangular bas-relief was created for the original wooden gate and was reinstalled in the new stone gate as well.

The building of the Museum of the Gas-Dynamic Laboratory

The shape of the attic of the St Peter Gate is reminiscent of the attic of the eastern façade of the Sts Peter and Paul Cathedral.

A very interesting episode in the history of Soviet science and technology has close connection with the St John Ravelin and half-counterguard of the Menshikov Bastion. In 1932—33 this was the site of experimentation and workshops for the first Soviet laboratory to create and develop rocket engines — the Gas-Dynamic Laboratory of the Military-Scientific Research Committee. This laboratory became the basis for the Experimental Design Bureau, where high-powered rocket engines were created which launched artificial satellites into orbit around the Earth, Moon and Sun, as well as launching the remote-controlled spaceships "Vostok", "Voskhod" and "Soyuz", and delivering automated stations to the Moon, Venus and Mars. Today the half-counterguard of the Menshikov Bastion houses the Museum of the Gas-Dynamic Laboratory.

After passing under the arch of the St Peter Gate, where one can still observe the signs of the former guides along which a grate was formerly lowered to block the path more securely, one sees the start of the main avenue of the fortress (whose full perspective is impeded by the central part of the main building of the Mint Works). Stepping out into the avenue, a one-storey pink-and-white building with a high gabled roof commands one's attention. It was built in 1748—49 for various offices of the Engineering Department, and this accounts for its name, the Engineers' House. This is a rare example of a St Petersburg military structure built in the 1740s which has preserved its original exterior appearance almost without change. Considerably less imposing in its outward appearance is the long one-storey building located on the other side of the avenue opposite the Engineers' House. It was built in 1801—2 as a storeroom for artillery, and towards the end of the nineteenth — beginning of the twentieth centuries was used as a manège. Walking further down the avenue past the Engineer' House and the artillery storeroom, one soon sees another two buildings to the left. One of them, the small two-storey yellow-and-white building with corners decorated with rusticated masonry and a portico in which two pairs of columns support a triangular pediment, stands almost directly next to the Neva Curtain Wall and separated from the main avenue by a large lawn. The other is also two-storey, though somewhat larger, red-and-white, and located a bit further back behind a lane which cross-cuts the main avenue. To one's right can be found the central architectural complex of the fortress, which includes two structures, built at different times and joined by a covered walkway: the Sts Peter and Paul Cathedral (standing directly next to the sidewalk of the main

avenue) and the Grand Ducal Burial Vault (separated from the main avenue by a small garden bordered by a low metal fence).

The yellow-and-white building served before the October Revolution of 1917 as the Main Guardhouse. It's present appearance is the result of reconstruction in the style of Classicism which took place in 1907—8 on the formerly one-storey stone guardhouse built in 1750.

The large lawn located to the left of the main lane, from the eighteenth to the beginning of the twentieth centuries, was the site of the fortress drill ground.

Before the Revolution the red-and-white building (its pedimented façade executed in the Baroque style faces the Engineers' House) was the residence of the fortress commandants, appointed from among the most distinguished generals of the Russian army. Hence its name — the Commandant's House. The first stone Commandant's House was built in 1748; at that time also a two-storey structure, but quite a bit smaller in size than the present house. In the years to follow, the Commandant's House was enlarged and rebuilt several times.

←

The main fortress avenue

The Engineers' House

It received its present dimensions and exterior view in 1893—94.
On October 24, 1917, in the Commandant's House the field headquarters for the direction of an armed uprising against the Provisional Government was established, acting on the decision of the Petrograd Military-Revolutionary Committee.
Today on display in the Commandant's House is an exhibition devoted to the history of St Petersburg — Petrograd up to February 1917. Among the items exhibited here, of particular interest are the old engravings, lithographs and paintings with images of the city, the works by leading Russian and foreign masters: Alexei Zubov, Mikhail Makhayev, John Augustus Atkinson, Benjamin Paterssen, Fiodor Alexeyev, Michel François Damame-Demartrais, Stepan Galaktionov, Karl Joachim Beggroff, Ferdinand Victor Perrot, Adolphe Charlemagne, Wilhelm Georg Timm, Anna Ostroumova-Lebedeva, Pavel Shillingovsky, and others.

The Main Guardhouse

The Commandant's House

In the very first years of the fortress on the site of today's Commandant's House stood a large building which served as the Main Guardhouse, and nearby, on the site of today's large lawn located to the left of the main fortress avenue, was the so-called "dancing square". Here, according to a contemporary, "a big wooden horse was installed with a very sharp spine, on which as a punitive measure soldiers were made to sit for several hours," and besides this "there was a wooden post sunk into the ground in front of which sharp spikes were installed, and above the post was a chain... When someone was being punished, his hands were locked into this chain, and the guilty was made to stand on those spikes for a time."

drum — that part of a building in the shape of a hollow-cylinder covered overhead with a dome which provides the interior of the building with natural overhead lighting

cupola — the curved, most often semi-circular, overhead covering of a drum

spire — the decorative detail crowning a building in the form of an extended upward-reaching pyramid

→

View of the cathedral from the east

The Sts Peter and Paul Cathedral is one of the most interesting monuments of Baroque architecture. Its general shape is that of an elongated rectangle stretching from west to east; its eastern portion is topped by a drum crowned by a cupola, its western portion is surmounted by a bell-tower with a tall spire. If one looks closely at the exterior of the cathedral, one immediately notices that the two pairs of volutes of the western façade are less expressive and contrast sharply with the two fine volutes of the eastern façade. One can also see that several large metal spikes extrude on the attic of the eastern façade, and that the drum awkwardly cuts into the two-gabled roof. All of these are a result of the not completely successful restoration of the cathedral after the terrible fire which occurred there on April 29, 1756, when a bolt of lightning struck the spire of the cathedral bell-tower. Twice lightning had struck the Sts Peter and Paul Cathedral prior to 1756, but without such catastrophic results.

The building of the stone Sts Peter and Paul Cathedral began in 1712. The unknown author of a small book about St Petersburg published in 1718 in Frankfurt and Leipzig wrote: "I can't leave unmentioned the large church and tall tower which has begun to be built in the fortress. Judging by the models I have seen, this will be something marvellous, the likes of which cannot yet be found elsewhere in Russia. The tower is finished up to the rafters, it is of extraordinary height and good stone masonry... and good proportions... It was built by the Italian architect Trezzini. Since the wooden upper portion of the tower should be as high as the stone part, the tower will probably surpass in height all the towers of Germany. About the church one can say that it will have everything that can possibly be desired in a place where materials are difficult to acquire."

The cathedral, consecrated on June 29, 1733, was, prior to the fire of 1756, a building consisting of three basic parts, compositionally connected to one another but nevertheless clearly distinguishable. The first part comprised the church building itself, in the form of an elongated rectangle with a slightly narrower altar, likewise rectangular. It was covered by a roof with a complex profile. The eastern façade of the building was topped by an attic with a curved pediment and two large volutes, decorated with wooden sculptures and vases which were supported by metal spikes. The western façade was topped by an attic with a triangular pediment and two other large volutes; this façade was also decorated by a portico which contemporaries termed "splendid". As in all typical Baroque cathedrals the side façades — northern and southern — were considerably less elaborate. The second main part of the cathedral in 1733—56 was the drum, extending above the roof near the attic of the eastern façade and surmounted

portico — an awning above a window or door opening in a wall

Volutes of the cathedral's western façade

lantern — the small drum located below the dome

ball — decorative detail crowning a building in the shape of a sphere

by a cupola which was crowned with a lantern and helmet-shaped dome. The third part of the cathedral was the square bell-tower with a complex top consisting of two octagonal cupolas with lanterns, a tall octagonal spire, a ball atop the spire and a cross with a flying angel crowning the ball (all these upper structures rested on a wooden base). Although the western façade of the bell-tower was projected as the continuation of the western façade of the cathedral, visually, before the fire of 1756, the bell-tower was perceived as "sprouting" from behind the attic with the triangular pediment.

Conceived by a Swiss-Italian architect for whom Russia became a second homeland and executed by skilled Russian stone- and wood-workers, the Sts Peter and Paul Cathedral, in terms of its exterior composition, was thoroughly original and had no analogues anywhere else in the world. At the same time as regards separate parts of the pre-fire cathedral, it is not difficult to find very interesting parallels in famous European churches of the sixteenth through eighteenth centuries, outstanding as monuments of Baroque architecture. Thus, the design of the western façade of the cathedral was very similar to that of the main façades of the famous Roman Baroque churches of the sixteenth and seventeenth centuries — Il Gesù and St Ignazio (neither of these two churches has a bell-tower). The Heilig-Geistkirche in Bern, built in 1722—29, with its bell-tower rising above its main façade square in plan and crowned by an eight-sided cupola, lantern and spire, immediately calls to mind the Sts Peter and Paul Cathedral the way it looked originally. Interesting partial parallels with the original Sts Peter and Paul Cathedral are further revealed in the London churches of St Bride, St Mary-le-Strand and St Martin-in-the-Fields. The first was built by the famous

Detail of a page from the album of engravings titled *Map of the Capital City of St. Petersburg...* with a representation of the cathedral (The Russian Museum, Leningrad)

English architect Sir Christopher Wren in the years 1670—1703; the second and third were built by the Scotsman James Gibbs in 1714—17 and in 1722—26, respectively. Just as the above-mentioned church in Bern, above each of these three London churches there rises a square-shaped bell-tower, and in the churches of St Bride and St Martin-in-the-Fields the bell-tower is crowned by an octagonal lantern and spire. It is interesting to note that since the Church of St Martin-in-the-Fields (considered to be the most outstanding of James Gibbs' works) served as a model for many churches built in the eighteenth century in the United States of America, similarities may be found between the original Sts Peter and Paul Cathedral and a whole array of architectural monuments in that country, for instance the small St Paul's Chapel in New York, built from the 1760s to the 1790s according to the plans of Thomas McBean. It should be added that in the original Sts Peter and Paul Cathedral the plan of the church building itself, as in all the above-mentioned foreign churches, is basilical, that is in the shape of an elongated rectangle, and that the spire as a decorative element was used widely in medieval architecture in Northern Europe.

But one must not forget to mention a St Petersburg forerunner and partial analogue to the Sts Peter and Paul Cathedral, the Church of the Resurrection, built on Vasilyevsky Island when it belonged to Alexander Menshikov, the first governor of the new Russian province, the centre of which became St Petersburg. The Church of the Resurrection, consecrated on November 23, 1713, and disassembled in 1730, was noted, in the words of its viewers, for its "handsome architecture" and "lovely tower" bearing a striking resemblance to the cathedral's bell-tower.

During the 1756 fire the wooden roof of the Sts Peter and Paul Cathedral burned completely,

Detail of the 1725 drawing titled *The Palace of His Highness Prince Menshikov*, with a representation of the Church of the Resurrection on Vasilyevsky Island (Library of the USSR Academy of Sciences, Leningrad)

→

A "mirror" image of the southern façade of the cathedral and cross-section of the cathedral published in the album of lithograph prints *Collection of Plans, Façades and Cross-sections of Noteworthy Buildings of St Petersburg*, published in 1826 in St Petersburg by the Society for the Encouragement of Artists (The Russian Museum, Leningrad)

as well as the cupola above the drum, the sculptures on the eastern façade and the entire complex structure surmounting the bell-tower. The portico of the western façade was also destroyed. In the years 1756—79 the cathedral was restored, but not to its exact former appearance. Above the church building proper a low gable roof now appeared, and the drum seems to cut crudely into it from above. The lantern above this drum became crowned with an ancient Russian onion-shaped cupola, fashionable in the mid-eighteenth century. The sculptures and vases of the eastern façade were not reconstructed, though, and the spikes supporting them before the fire were not removed. The Empress Catherine II personally saw to it in 1766 that the cathedral bell-tower be rebuilt "exactly as it was before". Indeed, in terms of general silhouette, proportions and architectural decorations, the restored bell-tower is very close to the original. However, the western attic with a triangular pediment was not restored — it was replaced by two pairs of crude flat volutes. As a result, the western façade of the bell-tower began to be visually perceived as a continuation of the cathedral's western façade, and the effect was lost of the bell-tower "sprouting" out from behind the attic with the triangular pediment. Now the cathedral ceased to be as clearly divided into three main parts as it was prior to the fire.

The restoration work on the cathedral bell-tower carried out in 1769—79 attracted widespread attention. One interesting account of this can be found in *Zhivopisets* (*The Painter*) — the satirical magazine which was published in 1772—73 by the famous Russian social figure and writer Nikolai Novikov. The hero of one of his satires, a provincial landowner, asks his son: "Write, dear Falaleyushka, what's going on there in Piter:

ПЛАНЪ ФАСАДЪ И
Plan,

авловскаго Собора

cathédrale

Paul.

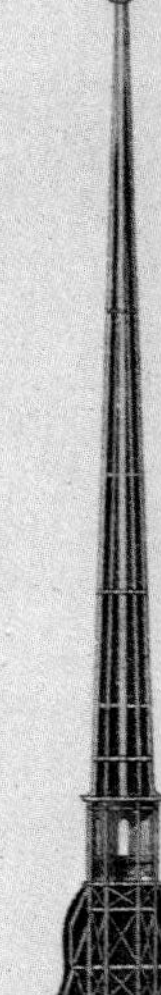

Сажени

Сажень

they say, great endeavours are undertaken. They're building a bell-tower and want it to be higher than Ivan the Great's (the famous bell-tower in the Moscow Kremlin)."

Speaking of the cathedral's bell-tower, one is always reminded of the story of how in 1830 the roofer Piotr Telushkin carried out repairs on the cross and the angel atop it. Famed for his great physical strength, Telushkin climbed out onto the exterior of the spire through a small window in one of its eight sides, and holding on with only his hands and toes to the grooves between the squares of gold leaf on the spire's ribs, he succeeded in encircling the entire spire, drawing a light rope behind him, and thus creating a rope loop. Now, by moving the loop upward and using hooks driven into some of the metal sheets, he was able to climb to the foot of the cross, from which he fastened a rope ladder extending back down to the window. With the help of the ladder he was able to

Soldiers raising the new bell to be installed in the cathedral bell-tower and observers watching the process. In the background at the left is the Mint Works, at the right the St Nicholas Curtain Wall with the St Nicholas Gate. Beginning of the 20th century (Central Archives of the Film-, Phono- and Photo-documents, Leningrad)

The raising of a new bell to be installed in the badly neglected bell-tower. Beginning of the 20th century (Central Archives of the Film-, Phono- and Photo-documents, Leningrad)

climb easily to his "workplace" under the clouds and carry out the repair work.

In the middle of the nineteenth century restoration work was once again carried out on the Sts Peter and Paul Cathedral. But this time its outer appearance remained unchanged. The badly weathered spire, lantern, and the cupola of the bell-tower, whose frameworks were of wood, were replaced in 1857—58 with replicas identical in form, but made of brick, dolomite and steel. At the same time and of the same long-lasting materials, the wooden lantern and dome of the cathedral's cupola were rebuilt preserving their previous form, and the roof was partially replaced as well.

Little has survived of the cathedral's original exterior architectural decorations. These include

platband — the frame of a window or door opening in a wall

the pilasters supporting the mighty entablature, running around the entire building, the simple platbands of the large rectangular windows with moulded cherubs at the tops, and the moulded frame of the oval window in the eastern façade depicting clouds and cherubs. After observing the inside of the cathedral one will see that the image of cherubs constitutes one of the most characteristic decorative details of the cathedral interior as well.

As regards the modest porticoes above the western and southern doors of the cathedral, they appeared after the fire of 1756. The large image of Christ and the Apostles Peter and Paul, located in the attic above the eastern façade decorated with two splendid volutes, was created in 1873.

Just as in the eighteenth century, the attention of viewers of the cathedral exterior is drawn to the bell-tower with its extraordinarily elegant spire (the overall height of the bell-

The Commandants' Cemetery. Seen acros the path to the left is the Commandant's House

Tombstone on the oldest grave in the Commandants' Cemetery, where the Scotsman Robert Bruce was buried, Head-commandant of the St Petersburg Fortress in the years 1704—20

chimes — in tower clocks, a mechanism attached to the clockworks which causes the bells to ring at a predetermined time

tower is 122.5 metres). And the clock and chimes mounted in the bell-tower attract no less attention. They were made in Holland, in 1757—60, by the talented craftsman Barend Oort Krass. The clock and chimes have been restored on several occasions, for instance in 1857—58 when the spire, cupola and lantern of the bell-tower were replaced. During the restoration of the clock face, which took place in the same period, the bell-tower clock was provided for the first time with a minute hand. Prior to this, the lack of the minute hand in this main clock of the city was compensated by short chimes, ringing every quarter of an hour. And today, just as earlier, on the fourth ringing of the chimes within an hour a different hour chime rings out. Nowadays, in addition, the clock chimes ring out the Soviet National Anthem four times a day: at 6 a.m., midday, 6 p.m., and midnight. Near the eastern façade of the cathedral a small eighteenth-century graveyard has been preserved. Up to the beginning of the twentieth century the fortress commandants were buried here.

A covered walkway leads from the cathedral and connects it to the Grand Ducal Burial Vault — the Church of St Alexander Nevsky (the patron saint of St Petersburg), consecrated on November 23, 1908, and built specially for burial of members of the Romanov dynasty (by the end of the nineteenth century there was no longer any room to bury family members in the Sts Peter and Paul Cathedral). The overall height of the Burial Vault is approximately sixty meters. Its square-shaped central part, covered overhead with a big vault, is surmounted with a drum, dome, lantern and small onion-shaped cupola. The eastern side of the central part is adjoined by a rectangular altar; next to the western side is a rectangular vestibule. The façades of the Burial Vault are more

Decoration of the façade of the Grand Ducal Burial Vault

←

The Grand Ducal Burial Vault

ornate than those of the cathedral; they are decorated with pilasters, half-columns, vases, volutes, mosaic icons and sculptured images of cherubs; likewise richly ornate are the vaulted ceiling and oval windows in it, as well as the drum, dome and lantern.

The Grand Ducal Burial Vault, whose architectural style may be termed eclectic, was built in 1897—1906 according to the design of David Grimm, Anton Tomishko and Leonty Benois. The three architects successfully selected the building site and height of the structure and likewise intentionally made the top of its dome similar to that of the cupola of the Sts Peter and Paul Cathedral. As a result, the silhouettes of the cathedral and the Burial Vault harmonize with one another and with the entire architectural complex of the fortress.

After viewing the exterior of the Sts Peter and Paul Cathedral one may enter it through its western doors, that is, from the side of Cathedral Square.

nave — the lengthwise part of a cathedral located between two rows of pylons or between a row of pylons and an exterior wall

pylon — a massive cross-shaped pillar

groin (cross) vault — complex overhead covering above that portion of the interior space of a building, formed by two crossed bow-shaped arches supported by four walls

in an Orthodox church, the middle part refers to its central part; adjacent to the middle part on its eastern side is the altar — the eastern part of a church with a communion table in its centre (usually narrower and slightly raised in relation to the middle part, and separated from the latter by the iconostasis — a barrier decorated with icons); adjacent to the middle part on its western side is the vestibule — the western part of a church (usually narrower than the middle part and sometimes separated from the middle part by a wall with doors); the communion table in an Orthodox church is a table for the performance of religious ceremonies, canopy — the name for a richly decorated awning (above the communion table, for example)

Interior of the Sts Peter and Paul Cathedral

Inside the cathedral impresses one first of all with the sheer size of the church hall, divided into three naves by two rows of pylons. The pylons support the square pieces of the mighty entablature, upon which rest the great arches, which in their turn serve as the support for the groin vaults and the pendentives under the drum. The central nave is somewhat wider than the side naves. The drum, pierced with windows and crowned with the cupola, towers above the central nave between the fourth and fifth (from the cathedral's western entrance) pairs of pylons. Along the cathedral walls are pilasters corresponding to the pylons. The pilasters support the mighty entablature extending along all the walls (except the transversal western wall at the back). This entablature which borders the cathedral inside is located at the same height as the pieces of the entablature which rest on the pylons, and has the same decorative pattern; it serves as a base for the arches which support the groin vaults.

The iconostasis is an integral part of the cathedral interior and divides it into two cross-sections, the middle part and the altar, above which spans the altar canopy.

The overall composition of the cathedral interior, in accordance with the basic precepts of Baroque church architecture, was intended to attract the viewer forward towards the iconostasis and altar, illuminated by rays of light from the cupola above. This composition has many parallels in Italian, Swiss and Southern German Baroque churches of the seventeenth and eighteenth centuries.

The cathedral is considerably more ornate on the inside than on the outside. The final stage

A ceiling painting in the central nave

in its construction coincided with the return of the Empress Anna I (Anna Ioannovna) from Moscow to St Petersburg, chosen once and for all as the permanent residence of the court. At the beginning of the 1730s, on the Empress Anna's orders, the cathedral interior was finished off more luxuriously than was called for in the original architectural plans. This luxurious interior has survived all subsequent remodelling.

The pylons and pilasters of the cathedral are painted to imitate green and pink marble, and they are crowned with gilt capitals adorned with cherubs. The vaults of the central nave

A ceiling painting in the right nave

are decorated with ceiling paintings depicting cherubs and angels holding the instruments of torture with which Christ was made to suffer before his death; the vaults of the side naves are decorated with ceiling paintings portraying angels holding objects used in the Orthodox bishop's worship service, and large eight-pointed stars. In addition, the vaults are decorated with ornamental edges, painted designs, and panels of various shapes. The vaults preserve the appearance they obtained in the 1870s. From them hang five large crystal chandeliers. In the pendentives under the drum decorated with corbels, pilasters and entabla-

pendentive — a triangular-shaped construction supporting the base of a drum

corbel — a decorative detail in the form of a support fixed into a wall

praporets — decorative detail imitating a small valance of elaborate shape with dangling tassels

ture, on which rests the cupola vault which covers the drum overhead, are moulded images of flying angels holding curtains which are dropping from above. The base of the drum is embellished with large images of cherubs, painted designs, and *praportsy,* valance-type decorations; and the drum itself. The paintings, arranged in two tiers in the drum, were created in 1877. The eight paintings of the bottom tier portray scenes from various Gospel stories, and the eight paintings of the top tier portray the Old Testament forefathers. The ceiling painting in the cupola depicts the Holy Spirit in the form of a dove encompassed by a bright aura radiating outward. It was painted in 1756—57, and was subsequently restored many times.

On the walls of the cathedral, underneath the arches of the vaults, eighteen large pictures can be found with scenes from the New Testament (on all the walls, except for the western one, these paintings seem to "stand" on the entablature encircling the inside of the cathedral). The paintings located on the side walls of the middle part of the cathedral and on the side walls of the altar are placed in moulded decorative frames, which, according to their design, were undoubtedly intended to match the attic of the cathedral's eastern façade. The picture on the eastern wall of the altar is placed in a frame richly decorated with moulded images of clouds, light rays radiating outward from the picture, and flying angels. The pictures on the remaining walls are without stuccoed framing. Seven of the eighteen pictures now located under the arches of the vaults were painted in 1728—31 by three artists: Vasily Ignatyev, Andrei Matveyev (both Russians), and Georg Gsell (a Swiss). Thanks to their realistic treatment, new to Russia in the eighteenth century, the pictures painted by these artists are considered outstanding in the history of

←

A pendentive under the drum

altarpiece — in a Catholic or Protestant church, a large sculpted or painted image located behind the altar; in these churches the altar refers to the table for performing religious ceremonies located in a portion of the church slightly upraised and opposite the main entrance

icon-case — a small, lavishly decorated wall or free-standing cabinet without front doors in which icons are displayed; in an iconostasis, a pedestal on which rests a large icon in an ornate frame. Among the decorative elements of the icon-case itself there may also be found icons of a smaller size

Holy Doors — the central doors of the iconostasis

northern doors — the doors in an iconostasis located to the left of the Holy Doors

southern doors — the doors of an iconostasis located to the right of the Holy Doors

Russian painting. The remaining eleven pictures are associated with the period from the second half of the 1750s to the beginning of the 1780s (they replaced paintings which were damaged in the fire of 1756) and are less interesting than the seven previously mentioned. Besides the eighteen pictures mentioned above, on the eastern wall of the altar under the oval window the large painted altarpiece is located.

The best decorations of the cathedral interior are the iconostasis and the altar canopy, donated to the cathedral by Peter the Great and his spouse and successor to the Russian throne, Catherine I. The general design of the iconostasis and altar canopy was drawn up by Trezzini, but they were executed in 1722—27 in Moscow out of soft limewood (lime-trees did not grow at that time in St Petersburg or its environs) under the direction of the architect Ivan Zarudny, who independently worked out the details of Trezzini's design. The iconostasis and altar canopy were delivered to St Petersburg in pieces and installed in the cathedral in 1729. Forty-three icons for the iconostasis and icons for the altar canopy were painted in St Petersburg in 1727—29 by a group of Moscow icon-painters summoned to St Petersburg especially for that purpose and headed by Andrei Merkulyev.

The basic composition of the iconostasis of the Sts Peter and Paul Cathedral consists of five large icon-cases, four arranged below and one situated above them. Located in the spaces between the four lower icon-cases are the Holy Doors, which correspond to the central nave; the northern doors, which correspond to the left nave; and the southern doors, which correspond to the right nave. A majestic arch stretches above the Holy Doors. Above the arch the fifth, upper, icon-case is located, extending into the space be-

←

The upper icon-case of the iconostasis

tween the drum and the cupola and reaching a height of almost twenty metres. The iconostasis is richly decorated with carvings and gilt from top to bottom. Altogether, in the icon-cases are located five large and thirty-six smaller icons; two additional large icons are placed on the northern and southern doors. Although the icon-cases of the iconostasis, if considered separately, remind one of the altarpieces of Baroque Catholic churches of the seventeenth and eighteenth centuries, the iconostasis as a whole is unparalleled anywhere in the world. Furthermore, similar iconostases had not existed in Russia before this one, with the possible exception of certain parts, also reminiscent of Catholic altarpieces, of the carved iconostasis in the aforementioned St Petersburg Church of the Resurrection which stood in 1713—30 on Vasilyevsky Island. (The author of the description of St Petersburg published in Frankfurt—Leipzig in 1718 mentions that in the Church of the Resurrection "there are several carved wooden sculptures and something like an altar, although this is not customary with the Russians.")

And indeed iconostases in Russian Orthodox churches of the seventeenth century looked little like the iconostasis in the Sts Peter and Paul Cathedral. They consisted of a wall, with the Holy Doors in the centre and northern and southern doors on either side. On this wall icons were arranged in horizontal tiers in a strictly determined order.

On the Holy Doors of Russian iconostases of the seventeenth-century six icons were invariably placed: two portrayed the Virgin Mary listening to the announcement of the Incarnation and the announcing Archangel Gabriel; the other four represented the four Evangelists. The Holy Doors of the iconostasis of the Sts Peter and Paul Cathedral were completely different. First of all, there is not even a single icon on them — they consist of

rotunda — a round structure whose essential parts are columns or pylons arranged in a circle and the cupola which they support

four wings with a bas-relief depicting the Last Supper taking place in a rotunda under a cupola pierced with round windows. The cupola of the rotunda is crowned with the image of crossed keys — a symbol of the Apostle Peter. Participants of the Last Supper are depicted on their way to the table standing in the centre of the rotunda; above the table, in an oval frame, the Virgin Mary is depicted, and above her the Holy Spirit in the form of a dove. To the left of the Holy Doors, on a high pedestal is the statue of the announcing Archangel Gabriel with a branch, and to the right of the Holy Doors, on a similar pedestal, is its pendant, a statue of the Archangel Michael fighting a dragon. Michael is holding a sword in the form of a long tongue of flame and a shield with the monogram of Christ.

A portion of one of the lower tiers of large icons in the iconostasis with an image of the Apostle Peter

In traditional Russian iconostases each horizontal tier of icons represented certain specific themes. With regard to themes, the arrangement of the iconostasis of the Sts Peter and Paul Cathedral is completely different: the iconostasis divides into the central part with the Holy Doors below; the southern (right) part, which may be named the "men's" section, for in it of the seventeen minor icons thirteen represent "holy men" (that is, heroes); and the northern (left) part, which may be named the "women's" section, for in it thirteen of the seventeen minor icons represent "holy women" (that is, heroines). Apparently this type of arrangement of the iconostasis was to serve as a reminder of those who donated it — the "hero" Peter I and "heroine" Catherine I.

True, in the iconostasis of the Sts Peter and Paul Cathedral it is possible to pick out a row of six large icons corresponding to the lowermost tier of icons in traditional Russian iconostases of the seventeenth century. However, only the location of the large image of Christ and the Apostle Peter to the right of the Holy

←

The Holy Doors of the iconostasis. Behind them, the canopy above the communion table

A sculptural representation of the Archangel Michael striking a dragon, one of the many sculptures decorating the iconostasis

Doors, the large image of the Mother of God and the Apostle Paul to the left of these doors, and the large image of the Prophet Ezekiel on the northern doors is in accordance with rules determining the arrangement of icons in seventeenth-century Russian iconostases. The large image of the Judge Samson bearing the city gates, located on the southern doors, is highly unusual for Russian seventeenth-century iconostases. The presence of the seventh large icon (depicting the Resurrection) in the upper icon-case of the iconostasis of the Sts Peter and Paul Cathedral does not contradict the rules for the selection of icons in former iconostases, but the placement of this image above the Holy Doors is again completely non-traditional.

Among the characters of the twenty-six icons depicting "holy men" and "holy women", interesting groups are notable. First of all these are certain members of the House of Rurik, who ruled Rus from 862 to 1598, the Saints Olga, Vladimir, Boris, Gleb, Alexander Nevsky and Dmitry Ioannovich. Next are the saints after whom Peter I's spouse and certain members of his family and relatives were named: Catherine, Natalia, Elizabeth, Praskovya and Anna. Further are the following saints: the Roman Emperor Constantine, his mother Helen and the Roman Empress Pulkheria. And finally, there are twelve Old Testament figures, the images of two of which appear in this iconostasis either for the first time ever, or are at least extremely rare in the history of Russian icon-painting. These are Bathsheba and Jael.

Bathsheba was the wife of the Hittite Uriah, a military leader of ancient Israel in the reign of King David. Having seen the lovely Bathsheba while bathing, David ordered his servants to lead her to him that night in the palace. Later David sent Uriah to his head commander, having secretly ordered the latter: "Set ye

Uriah in the forefront of the hottest battle, and retire ye from him, that he may be smitten, and die." Uriah was killed in battle, and David made Bathsheba his wife. The Old Testament author ends his description of the actions of the King with this commentary: "But the thing that David had done displeased the Lord." However, the author didn't pass judgement on Bathsheba.

Long before this story another one took place, the heroine of which was a woman from the Palestinian tribe of the Kenites by the name of Jael. During one of the wars of the ancient Israelites in Palestine, one of the thwarted opponents, the Canaanite military leader Sisara sought refuge in Jael's home. When the exhausted man fell asleep in Jael's tent, she "took a nail of the tent, and took an hammer in her hand, and went softly unto him, and smote the nail into his temples, and fastened it into the ground..." Jael's actions were lauded by the prophetess Deborah, who was the leader of the Israelites at that time.

The image of Samson on the southern doors of the iconostasis

Neither Bathsheba nor Jael were considered saints by the Orthodox Church. Why then in the late 1720s did their images appear in the iconostasis of the main Orthodox shrine in St Petersburg? There seems to be only one answer to this question: it must have been some peculiar form of apology for Catherine I, for whom Peter the Great was not the first husband — just as David for Bathsheba, and who, in the eyes of the Russians, remained a foreigner — like Jael for the ancient Jews.

The majority of icons in the cathedral iconostasis are painted in a realistic manner. Especially noteworthy in this respect are the images of Deborah and Esther (located in the "women's" left half, up above, in frames suggestive of a flower with three petals) and the landscape which is the background for the depiction of the Apostles Peter and Paul.

The iconostasis has relief images of the regalia

The images of Deborah (three-leafed) and St Olga (oval) in the "holy women's" half of the iconostasis

of the Russian emperors — the crown and sceptre (they can be seen on the side walls of the four lower icon-cases and on the cupola of the rotunda of the Holy Doors).

There are many inscriptions on the iconostasis, the script of which is suggestive of those in St Peter's Cathedral in Rome. Therefore, in the inscriptions of the iconostasis in place of the Cyrillic *B* and *У* the Latin letter *V* is used, and the Cyrillic *H* is replaced by the Latin *N*.

Major restorations of the iconostasis in the eighteenth and nineteenth centuries made virtually no changes in its original appearance.

In May 1756 it was again reassembled after being hastily dismounted on April 30 and rescued from the burning cathedral. In 1832—33, to protect the iconostasis from dampness, a marble socle was installed beneath it. In 1865—66 the deteriorated wooden Holy Doors were replaced with exact copies embossed in copper and covered with gold.

In the centre of the altar above the communion table and exquisitely fitting into the arch of the Holy Doors, the carved wooden altar canopy stands on four twisted columns. Its prototype is one of the best works of the famous Italian architect and sculptor, Gian-

The image of St Constantine above the southern doors of the iconostasis

lorenzo Bernini, the splendid bronze canopy of St Peter's Cathedral in Rome, installed there in 1633.

pulpit — in Orthodox, Catholic and Protestant churches, a raised place near a wall, pylon or column from which the sermon is read

On the fourth pylon on the left a carved wooden pulpit is fixed, above which a canopy is suspended. Several wooden sculptured images decorate the pulpit: the Apostles Peter and Paul above the canopy; the four Evangelists and their "living symbols" (St Matthew with an angel, St Mark with a lion, St Luke with a bull, and St John with an eagle) and the Holy Spirit in the form of a dove, surrounded by clouds and cherubs on the canopy itself. Paintings decorate the pulpit as well. Among them of special interest, due to its life-like quality, is one picture illustrating the famous Evangelical parable of the sower. Of the fine details of the canopy over the pulpit, it is worthwhile to note the valance-type decorations similar to those which adorn the base of the drum and the altar canopy. As to the use of the pulpit for reading sermons, it first appeared in the Orthodox churches of St Petersburg in the same Church of the Resurrection mentioned earlier. The author of the description of 1718, when speaking of the sermons read from the pulpit of this church, emphasized: "This is something new and out of the ordinary, since formerly the Russians didn't read a sermon, but conducted only a worship service."

Near the fourth pylon on the right in the cathedral is the place designated for the Emperor, a small low platform on which the Emperor stood while attending the church service. Above this platform a carved wooden canopy is located with the image of the Imperial insignia (crown, sceptre and sword) resting on pillows. Curtains of crimson-coloured velvet hang from the canopy; on the back curtain covering the pylon the State Eagle is embroidered. Judging by the peculiarities of the latter, it is possible to assume that the place designated for the Emperor, the creator

Decoration of the canopy above the communion table. At the right, a monogram with the Imperial crown above it

of which is unknown, acquired its present appearance no earlier than the beginning of the 1830s and no later than the mid-1850s, since the rider on the Moscow coat-of-arms, located on the eagle's breast, is turned to the heraldic left side (as portrayed only up to 1856), and on the eagle's wings are the coats-of-arms of Kazan, Astrakhan, Siberia, Poland, Chersonesus and Finland (these coats-of-arms appeared on the State Eagle in 1832).

Today in the middle part of the Sts Peter and Paul Cathedral are located thirty-two grave tombs of members of the Romanov dynasty, but actually buried here are only thirty-one, since the monument for the Grand Duchess Alexandra Georgiyevna, daughter of the Greek King George I, stands above an empty grave: the coffin with Alexandra Georgiyevna's remains was returned by the Soviet Govern-

ment to Greece in 1939 for reburial in the Royal Burial Vault in Athens. Eleven of the thirty-one buried here were ruling Russian emperors and empresses of the Romanov dynasty. They include those having died in the eighteenth century: Peter the Great, Catherine I, Anna I, Elizabeth I, Peter III and Catherine II (in the right nave); and those having died in the nineteenth century: Paul I, Alexander I, Nicholas I, Alexander II and Alexander III (in the left nave).
Thirty of the thirty-two tombstones are of white marble with gilt bronze plaques bearing the name of each of those buried, their title,

←
Canopy above the pulpit

The Imperial seat. In the background, at the right, the pulpit with canopy above it

date of birth and death, etc. Furthermore, the image of the State Eagle is fixed to the corners of the monuments on the graves of the ruling emperors of Russia and likewise to those of their spouses (formally considered co-rulers).

Prior to 1844 only a portion of the graves in the cathedral had low monuments above them. In 1844—65 the first white marble tombstones were installed above seven new graves as they appeared in the cathedral. In 1865—67 white marble tombstones replaced the majority of earlier monuments. The texts on the plaque of the new monument to Peter I and certain others were compiled by the eminent Russian historian Nikolai Ustrialov, the author of the ten-volume *History of the Rule of Peter the Great*, in which, in particular, for the first time documents were published in connection with the case of Prince Alexei, Peter's son, who died in the St Petersburg Fortress in 1718. Above the subsequent graves white marble tombstones were likewise installed, which, by the beginning of the twentieth century already numbered forty. However, ten of these were removed from the cathedral in 1906—8. Eight of the ten were removed and the remains transferred to the Grand Ducal Burial Vault built next to the cathedral. Two of the monuments near the northwest wall — above the graves of the Emperor Alexander II and his spouse Maria Alexandrovna — were replaced by new monuments differing greatly in form and material from all the others. The new monument to Alexander II was carved from a monolithic piece of wavy jasper from the Altai Mountains, and the new monument to Maria Alexandrovna of a monolith of pink quartz from the Urals. Carved in 1888—1906 according to the design of the architect A. Gun, they are splendid examples of the art of Russian stone-cutting of the turn of the century. In the vestibule, under the stairs leading to

→

This is the way the interior of the cathedral looked from the end of 1894 until the summer of 1917 when, at the order of the Provisional Government, all of its treasures were transferred to Moscow (Central Archives of the Film-, Phono- and Photo-documents, Leningrad)

the bell-tower, one may view three additional tombstones in the form of marble slabs embedded in the wall. One of the slabs marks the burial place of Prince Alexei, the only grown-up son of Peter the Great. In addition fastened to the wall in the middle part of the cathedral, near its northern doors, is a plaque with the names of Peter's five children who died as infants and were buried somewhere in this vicinity. In 1916, during World War I, attempts were made to use the graves in the Sts Peter and Paul Cathedral to ignite feelings of patriotism and support for the monarchy. Rumours spread in abundance around Petrograd of

Tombstone of Peter the Great. To the left of it, the tombstone of Catherine I; in the second row, nearer to the iconostasis, the tombstones of Anna I, Peter III and Catherine II

certain miracles alleged to have been witnessed near the grave monument of Paul I.
Today the burial sites in the Sts Peter and Paul Cathedral are preserved as historical monuments — the graves of famous statesmen of the past. The tomb of Peter the Great attracts the attention of all who visit the fortress.
As you finish viewing the inside of the cathedral, notice the banners hanging on the southern, western and northern walls; these are exact copies of some of those banners which hung before the Revolution in the middle part of the cathedral (banners captured as trophies by Russian troops during the wars with Sweden and Turkey in the eighteenth century).
It should be emphasized that the Sts Peter and Paul Cathedral is a unique example of the extraordinarily bold combination of Western European artistic imagery with the traditional distinctive features of Orthodox church architecture. It is a splendid monument not only of Russian, but of world art and culture as well. Furthermore, thanks to the richness of its interior décor, the cathedral constitutes a unique visual handbook for those interested in architecture and the monumental decorative nature of Baroque art.
The Cathedral of Sts Peter and Paul is of particular interest as an unusual example of the early period in the history of St Petersburg church architecture, demonstrating a unique blend of Eastern and Western church traditions.

Having viewed the cathedral inside, one may exit through its northern doors into a closed walkway. The walkway soon turns to the right towards the Burial Vault, and the doors on the left open into the small yard, which is separated from Cathedral Square by a lovely wrought-iron fence, created in 1904—6 by the architect Leonty Benois, who used as his model the famous wrought-iron work of the fence surrounding the Summer Gardens, St Petersburg's first garden-park.

Behind the fence, on Cathedral Square, is the Boathouse — a small fine Baroque pavilion on the roof of which stands a terracotta statue, the allegorical image of Navigation, created in 1891 by David Jensen. This pavilion, built in 1761 according to the design of the architect Alexander Vüst, was intended for the preservation of the "grandfather of the Russian Navy" — the above-mentioned famous boat which had been kept in 1723—61 in the kronwerk. Now the boat is on display in the Central Naval Museum located not far from the fortress on the spit of Vasilyevsky Island.

On the opposite side of Cathedral Square stands the building of the Mint Works. The central part of this building, designed in 1800—2

Wrought-iron fence of the garden in front of the western entrance to the Grand Ducal Burial Vault

The Boathouse

by the architect Antonio Porto in the style of Classicism, is crowned by a triangular pediment whose tympanum bears the State Emblem of the USSR; on the right and left the building is flanked by round towers with flattened domes.

The Mint Works, opened in the fortress in 1724, has remained the main centre of coin production in the Soviet times. Here in 1921 began the minting of the first Soviet silver coins, whose circulation played a vital role in battling inflation and economic devastation, widespread in the country after the Civil War of 1918—21. Here the first Soviet orders were also made. Since 1961 the Leningrad Mint Works has been producing coins of brass and *neusilber* which are in current circulation in the USSR. Since 1814 the Mint Works has enjoyed a

The Mint Works and Cathedral Square

monopoly on the production of Russian medals. Therefore, closely associated with it are the names of remarkable Russian medal-makers: Karl von Leberecht, Alexander Lialin, Fiodor Tolstoy, Pavel Utkin (whose works include several medals commemorating major events in the history of St Petersburg and Russia), and likewise the leading Soviet medallists of the 1920s and 1930s, Anatoly Vasiutinsky, N. Sokolov and others.

At the St Petersburg Mint Works was created a unique monument of the eighteenth-century Russian applied arts — the silver shrine for the relics of Prince Alexander Nevsky, which is now kept in the Hermitage Museum.

From the Boathouse the St Nicholas Curtain Wall and the St Nicholas Gate are readily visible. To the right of the curtain wall is

the Golovkin Bastion, in whose courtyard stands the cavalier, joined to the upper level of the curtain wall by a stone bridge. The façade of the cavalier, turned towards the inside of the Peter and Paul Fortress, is decorated with ornamental embrasures, hollow windows and a large hollow arch under which are two splendidly executed moulded images of lictor fasces.

The cavalier acquired its present form in the first half of the nineteenth century, after the rebuilding of the original structure into an artillery storehouse.

Passing through the St Nicholas Gate behind the St Nicholas Curtain Wall, the Kronwerk Strait is visible, on whose opposite shore stands the mighty building of the Defence Arsenal.

Sample coins and medals minted at the St Petersburg — Petrograd Mint Works prior to 1917: a 1724 rouble bearing the image of Peter the Great — the first rouble to be minted in St Petersburg; a 1757 five-copeck piece with the image of the St Petersburg coat-of-arms; a 1805 medal created to commemorate the laying of the cornerstone of the Stock Exchange building on Vasilyevsky Island bearing the image of this building; a 1807 rouble with the image of the "State Eagle" — the first rouble to be minted after reconstruction at the turn of the 18th and 19th centuries; a 1850 medal commemorating the completion of the first permanent bridge in St Petersburg, bearing the image of that bridge and the flying "State Eagle"; a 1896 medal with the image of the building of the St Petersburg Mint Works created as a gift to the Paris Mint Works; a 1914 rouble with the image of Peter I struck in commemoration of the 200th anniversary of the victory on the Hangö Peninsula; a 1915 rouble with the image of the "State Eagle" — the last rouble to be minted under the monarchy (The Hermitage Museum, Leningrad)

Sample coins, medals and plaques minted at the Petrograd—Leningrad Mint Works since 1921: a 1921 50-copeck piece with the image of the fivepointed star — one of the first Soviet coins; a 1924 rouble with the image of the worker and collective farmer; a 1926 plaque with the image of the Mint Works building; a 1937 medal created in commemoration of the 20-year anniversary of the October Revolution, with the image of the red guard and soldiers at Smolny; rouble, 50-copeck, 20-copeck, 15-copeck and 10-copeck pieces, all minted in 1967 in commemoration of the 50-year anniversary of Soviet power and bearing the image of the State Emblem of the USSR (on the rouble and 10-copeck pieces) Vladimir Ilyich Lenin, the cruiser *Aurora* and the sculpture *Worker and Collective Farmer;* a 1984 rouble created in commemoration of the 185th anniversary of the birth of Alexander Pushkin, bearing the image of the poet (The Hermitage Museum, Leningrad)

Cathedral Square. In the background, the St Nicholas Curtain Wall and St Nicholas Gate

View of the Defence Arsenal from the St Nicholas Curtain Wall

The junction of the right flank and orillon in the Zotov Bastion. The flank has been restored to show the original embrasures; the orillon shows the sortie as it appeared

To the right and left of the arsenal building, near the ends of its metal fences, two small granite bridges can be seen. The right bridge stretches across the source of the moat surrounding the kronwerk, the left crosses its mouth. The small pyramid-like cupola, which is visible behind the arsenal when standing at the St Nicholas Gate, crowns a building erected before the Revolution by the St Petersburg City Trusteeship for People's Sobriety — the so-called Folk House. This building is the closest site in the vicinity of the fortress which is associated with Lenin: twice — in 1917 and 1919 — Lenin gave major speeches here. To the right of the kronwerk stands the building of the Orthopedic Institute; to the left of the kronwerk one can see the facilities and structures of the Leningrad Zoo.

After exiting through the St Nicholas Gate the Zotov Bastion will appear on the viewer's left. Its right shoulder corner and the beginning of the orillon extending from it have been restored to the way they looked after the reconstruction of the earthen bastion into a stone structure. Here the sortie has been partially restored.

sortie — an opening in the wall of a permanent fortified structure for sallies of the besieged during battle

One may walk along the right face of the Zotov Bastion until coming to a wide opening in the batardeau, joining the salient angle of this bastion with the half-counterguard covering its left face. Having passed through this opening, one will soon find oneself between the Vasilyevsky Island Curtain Wall (in the centre of which is located the Vasilyevsky Island Gate) and the two-storey semi-circular building located inside the Alexei Ravelin (in this building, constructed in 1893—95, prior to the Revolution the archives of the chancellory and several main offices of the Ministry of

Semi-circular building which stands on the place of the Secret House

View of the Admiralty Embankment through the grate of the batardeau of the Trubetskoi Bastion

Defence were located.) From here the Trubetskoi Bastion and its batardeau are readily visible to the right of the Vasilyevsky Island Gate. Behind the batardeau is the Neva, on the opposite bank of which can be seen the Winter Palace, as well as the towering Main Admiralty Building and St Isaac's Cathedral. In the vicinity of St Isaac's Cathedral and the Admiralty, near *The Bronze Horseman*, a monument to Peter the Great, on December 14, 1825, stood the rebels' detachments.

The St Alexei Ravelin as well as the Zotov and Trubetskoi Bastions located as far as possible from the St Peter Gate, constitute not only one of the fortress' most "non-showy" places, but even one of its most gloomy components, i.e., the prison. Characteristically, neither the Zotov nor the Trubetskoi Bastions ever changed names, whereas of the four other bastions, three took on new, more "formal" names when Catherine I, Peter II, and Anna I came to the throne, respectively.

On the place of the yellow two-storey building, formerly occupied by archives, a one-storey stone building once stood, triangular in shape just like the ravelin — this was the Secret House (it was demolished in 1893). The Secret House was one of the most terrible political prisons of Tsarist Russia in 1797—1884. Its name, "Secret House", is no accident. The "last Decembrist" Dmitry Zavalishin, a naval officer and close associate of the organizers of the Uprising of December 14, 1825, who knew of its preparations and outlived all the other participants of the historic uprising, wrote that the Secret House was a "fortress within a fortress or, to use a popular expression, a stone bag", since those who came to be held there "were no longer called by their names, but rather by the cell numbers in which they were kept." Besides the Decembrists, the members of the Petrashevsky Circle, the "People's Will" and members of various anarchist groups were imprisoned here as well. In 1882 the revolutionary Sergei Nechayev died in the Secret House, a man seemingly cloaked in puzzling contradictions. Extraordinarily brave, and completely committed to the struggle against Tsarism, he possessed fantastic energy and the rare talent of influencing people. He became the only captive of the Secret House to succeed in winning the sympathy of the soldier guards who agreed to help him in an escape attempt. In a report on this incident the Emperor Alexander III could only write: "A more disgraceful event for the military command and its leaders, I think, has never taken place up to now." At the same time Nechayev lacked any moral principles whatsoever and believed it possible to resort to any provocation and any deceitful act. His methods repulsed many away from the revolutionary movement, among them the former prisoner of the same Secret House, the famous Russian writer Fiodor Dostoyevsky, arrested for participating in meetings of the the Petrashevsky Circle. After Nechayev's methods were revealed to the public in 1871 at an open political process in St Petersburg, the first trial of its kind to take place in Russia, Dostoyevsky wrote his famous novel *The Possessed*. The entire Russian revolutionary movement condemned Nechayev's methods,

Courtyard of the Zotov Bastion with the ramp for rolling big guns

and Karl Marx and Frederick Engels absolutely rejected the social structure advocated by Nechayev, which they termed "barracks communism", since its main points included the unlimited rule by certain groups of leaders and terror of the threat of execution as the basis to discipline the masses.

Having passed through the Vasilyevsky Island Gate, built in 1954 according to sketches of the gate which had been erected here in 1792—94 and disassembled in the mid-nineteenth century, the viewer will find himself on the narrow by-street between the Vasilyevsky Curtain Wall and the back side of the Mint Works.

If one follows this side-street to the left, it will lead to the inner courtyard of the Zotov Bastion. Casemates were built within the faces and ramps of this bastion which served on more than one occasion as the place of confinement of political prisoners. Thus certain participants of the Decembrist Uprising of 1825 were confined here. Three cannons remind us of the events which occurred on that day in St Petersburg. The government forces used this type of weapon in supressing the uprising.

If upon passing through the Vasilyevsky Island Gate one follows the small side-street to the right, it will lead to the gate located inside the rather non-descript two-storey building within the Trubetskoi Bastion. This is the other prison of the St Petersburg Fortress, enjoying a no less ominous reputation than the Secret House.

The Prisoners' Department in the St Petersburg Fortress (as the prison was officially called) was established in 1870—71. The prison is pentagonal in shape, following the configuration of the bastion in which it is built. The four exterior walls of the building face the inner side of the bastion walls at a distance of a mere three to four metres; the fifth exterior wall with a gate faces a corner of the Mint

The façade of the prison in the Trubetskoi Bastion

Works. Inside the prison is a small courtyard, in the centre of which is located the small one-storey convicts' bathhouse. A small exercise yard is also located here for the prisoners to walk in.

Only the windows of the corridor look out on the courtyard, and the windows, placed at different heights in the sixty-nine solitary confinement cells and two punishment cells, without exception looked out on the blank bastion walls. Only staff offices and rooms were located in that portion of the prison building which faced the corner of the Mint Works.

This building, lacking any architectural or cultural value, has been carefully preserved to commemorate the many outstanding activists of the revolutionary movement in Russia. Incarcerated here were those under investigation in cases of special political importance, as well as "political criminals, deprived of all civic rights and sentenced to exile to hard labour camps". Those convicted were confined here for a more or less lengthy period following sentencing before being sent to another prison, to place of exile, or execution.

The main method of inhumane psychological treatment of those held in the prison of the Trubetskoi Bastion was their total isolation from one another under conditions of strict silence in combination with their continual control and observation. The subsequently famous leader and theoretician of European Anarchism Prince Piotr Kropotkin, imprisoned here during the early years of the prison's existence, recalled: "Not a single sound reached us, with the exception of the footsteps of the guard, stealing by, like a hunter, from one door to another in order to peek through the small peep-hole windows in the doors, which we called 'Judas'. In fact you are never alone, you can always sense the watchful eye, and yet at the same time you are still in utter solitude."

Passage between the wall of the Trubetskoi Bastion and the wall of the prison building located within

Knocking on the walls was the only means of contact between those in neighbouring cells. But everything was done to deprive the prisoners of this possibility as well. The multi-layered insulation of the prison facilities has been exposed in one of the cells to demonstrate what measures were taken to prevent communication.

The building construction and reinforced guard both inside and outside made escape from this prison impossible.

The prison was especially hard on female prisoners. Many of them could not bear the severity of the prison regime and committed suicide. Thus, in 1897 one prisoner, the twenty-six-year-old Maria Vetrova, lit her clothing on fire after dousing them with kerosene from the small lamp provided in the cell, and died a few days later from severe burns.

Many prisoners of the Peter and Paul Fortress left behind memoirs which help understand what they suffered being cut off from the entire world, how they attempted to fight conditions which preyed not only on their bodies but on their minds and spirits as well.

Dmitry Akhsharumov, a participant in the meetings at Butashevich-Petrashevsky's, recalled the following about his stay in the Secret House: "The main thing which I would like to describe and explain is the tormented morbid inner state of one who has been held a long time without repose in solitary confinement, the feeling of severe anguish, the gloomy thoughts which tormented me continually, and at times of low spirits, to the point of losing my voice and utter breakdown. Day and night I talked to myself, and not receiving any response from the outside, I withdrew into myself, to the company of my own morbid imaginings."

"I greatly wanted", wrote one of the first proletarian revolutionaries, Alexander Shapovalov, prisoner of the Trubetskoi Bastion, "to break down these hated walls, to pull out the wrought-iron grate and be free once again. But the walls are strong. The iron is thick. The guards are vigilant. It's all in vain. One cannot get out of here."

One of the organizers of the assassination of Alexander II, the extraordinarily brave, resourceful and at the same time irreproachably honest and extremely modest, Mikhail Frolenko, who spent two and a half years in the Secret House and suffered terribly there along with his comrades from scurvy, which sent many of them to their graves, recalled: "There arose an especially acute fear for each individual life, especially for those about whom one could find out nothing... In every rustling, in each unusual sound, I imagined death, violence, horror. There appeared an unquenchable, tormenting urge to creep into another cell, to give the dying one an opportunity to spend even a minute with a friend... Suddenly the despairing cry of a dying human being broke the dead silence. The cry was followed by a short bustle of activity — a struggle, and one could hear something heavy being dragged through the corridor. What had happened? Who did they beat? Or who has gone crazy? The awareness of one's own helplessness brought tears to the eyes... There appeared a strong desire to break arms, to shout, to become violent, crack one's skull. But to what end?"

In 1883—84 a remarkable woman, member of the Executive Committee of "The People's Will", Vera Figner, was confined in the Trubetskoi Bastion. More than four decades later she wrote in her memoirs, one of the most interesting sources on the history of public life and social movements in Russia during the period from 1870 to the 1890s: "In the extreme situation when all customary outside impulses are cut off and disappear, the thought process, with all its power of stimulation,

turns inward and for the first time for me as well as probably for the majority of those imprisoned after long years of revolutionary activity and because of this activity, not having had leisure for self-introspection, I was forced to reconstruct in my mind my entire life — from the first moment of consciousness to the last minute of freedom; recall all the influences, all stages in my development as an individual, and then to review my years of participation in the revolutionary movement from the year '76 up to and including '83. This intense concentrated mental effort was, because of its novelty and content, attractive, interesting and productive. It is described in the statement written by me in place of a deposition; it is preserved in archives and helped me later to write the book *The Recorded Labour*."

Not a few of the opponents of Tsarism held in the Peter and Paul Fortress were at the same time leading representatives of Russian culture, not broken spiritually even under the inhumane conditions of solitary confinement. Fiodor Dostoyevsky, during his stay in the Secret House, wrote the short story *The Little Hero*.

The famous radical literary critic and author of numerous articles on economic and political questions, Nikolai Chernyshevsky, arrested in 1862 and accused of compiling anti-government appeals directed towards Russian peasants, was held in the Secret House until the showy public performance imitating his "civic execution" followed by his exile in 1864. Chernyshevsky was a staunch believer in Utopian Socialism, and even his most ardent opposers characterized him as a "creature purest in heart". Chernyshevsky wrote in prison his world-famous novel *What Is to Be Done?* — full of greatly optimistic pictures of a happy future life, the basis of which is to be peaceful, joyful and rational labour, which will lead to the formation of physically and morally perfect human beings. This novel had an immense influence on Russia's revolutionary youth of the 1860s and 1870s.

In 1862 one of the most determined representatives of the violent protest against the current social structure, the publicist and literary critic Dmitry Pisarev was confined in the fortress prison. He spent more than four years on Fortress Island. Fighting the overwhelming despair of solitude, Pisarev was allowed not only to write, but even to publish his works before regaining his freedom. In the fortress he wrote more than half of his works, and it was here that he evolved his theory of "strict and consistent realism", determined as "the economics of mental faculties".

Yet another outstanding individual whose cheerful spirit and intellectual energy couldn't be broken even by the Secret House was Nikolai Morozov, a member of "The People's Will". Morozov entered the Secret House in 1882 following his sentencing to life imprisonment in the fortress. "During the first half-year of imprisonment in the ravelin," he recalled, "we were given absolutely no books to read, and later... they gave us religious books. I devoured them greedily. This was a subject completely unexplored by me, and I immediately saw what rich food for thought ancient church literature can be for a rational mind already adequately acquainted with astronomy, geophysics, psychology and other natural sciences... During this time the plots came to me for my future books: *Revelation in Thunder and Storm*, *The Prophets* and several of the chapters included in the first and second volumes of my long work *Christ*."

Following the beginning of the First Russian Revolution several eminent Russian scientists, writers and social activists who tried to prevent the shooting on January 9, 1905, of a peaceful workers' demonstration in St Petersburg were confined in the prison of the Trubetskoi

Bastion. Among them was the already world-famous writer Maxim Gorky, who made an appeal on the evening of January 9 "To all Russian citizens and public opinion of all European governments". Gorky was released in a few weeks thanks to a widespread campaign in Russia and abroad in his defence. While in prison Gorky wrote the tragic comedy *Children of the Sun*, showing how far the Russian intelligentsia, "blind, drunk not with deeds, but only with pretty words and ideas", was from understanding the real needs of the Russian people.

In 1907 the tsarist authorities closed down the periodical journal *Byloye* (*The Past*) published in St Petersburg since January 1906 and dedicated to the history of the Russian liberation movement (which published, incidentally, on a regular basis news about prisoners of the "Russian Bastille"). One of its publishers, the historian and literary critic Piotr Shchogolev spent more than two years in the Peter and Paul Fortress, where he completed his great work *The Duel and Death of Pushkin*.

Leaving the prison facilities of the Trubetskoi Bastion, one may walk along the narrow street between the Catherine Curtain Wall and the Mint Works to the Naryshkin Bastion, upon which stands the flagstaff tower built in 1731—32. In the nineteenth century flags and the keys to the fortress gates were kept here. Today, two guns stand on the bastion to the right of the flagstaff tower. Everyday precisely at 12:00 noon one of them fires a blank shot (the second stands by on reserve). This old tradition was renewed during Leningrad's 250-year anniversary celebration.

Flagstaff tower

Not far from the Naryshkin Bastion is the Neva Gate, built in the style of Classicism by the architect Nikolai Lvov. The gate faces the fortress and is decorated with two pairs of pilasters and a triangular pediment under which the date of the gate's construction can be read — 1787. The tympanum of the pediment contains a cartouche similar to the one located on the St John Gate.

When you pass under the Neva Gate and walk towards the bank of the Neva, notice the marble and metal plaques fastened to the wall marking the maximum waterline in six places during the most severe floods of the Neva. These marks are accompanied by the following inscriptions:

November 7, 1824, in the second hour of the afternoon water stood 12 feet 10 inches above the normal water level as marked by the line between the letters A and B;

September 23, 1924, at 19:30 hours water stood 11 feet and 8 inches above the normal water level as indicated by this line;

September 10, 1777, in the seventh hour p.m. water stood according to the red line 9 feet and 11 inches above the normal water level;

September 29, 1975, from 3:55 a.m. to 4:20 a.m. water stood 9 feet and 4 inches above the normal water level as indicated by the line;

October 23, 1752, in the tenth hour p.m. according to the green line water stood 8 feet and 5 inches above the normal water level; September 27, 1788, in the second hour a.m. water stood according to the blue line 7 feet and 6 inches above the normal water level. To the left of these curious "chronicle of the floods of the Neva" fastened to the wall is a tide-gauge consisting of a surveyor's rod marked off in points, which serves to determine the height of water on the river.
The floods recorded here caused great damage to the entire city as well as to the fortress itself.
Exiting onto the Neva or Commandant's Pier, built in 1777, you will see first and foremost the splendid panorama of the Palace Embankment on the opposite bank. To the left across the Neva spans the Kirov (formerly the

View onto the Neva Gate from the fortress

The Chronicle of the Floods

Trinity) Bridge, the most beautiful bridge in Leningrad opened May 16, 1903, during the city's bicentennial celebration. Its street lights and obelisks standing near its ends remind one of the Alexander III Bridge in Paris, which was built in 1896 in commemoration of the expansion of Russian-French ties which had commenced five years earlier.

Not far from the pier on the right you will again see (this time from the outside) the Naryshkin Bastion. The Neva flows almost right up to its very feet, and the Bastion and the pier appear to be "emerging" out of the water. In the eighteenth century the entire fortress façade "emerged" out of the water in this way.

Behind the Naryshkin Bastion, in front of the Catherine Curtain Wall stand a few dozen tall trees not visible from the pier — the remnants of the park built in 1862 for exercising certain "noble" prisoners (that is, prisoners of noble descent). A little further along the bank of the Neva, and also not visible from the pier, are the Trubetskoi Bastion with the batardeau and half-counterguard and the St Alexei Ravelin. In the opposite direction from the pier stretches the Neva Curtain Wall which ends at the third bastion on the Neva side, the Tsar Bastion. Behind this bastion are located its batardeau and half-counterguard. The fortress walls facing the Neva are reveted with granite. The granite reveting of the Neva façade contains a number of decorative elements. The corners of the bastions, the half-counterguard and the ravelin are rusticated, and small towers rise exquisitely above these corners.

At the end of the eighteenth century the Neva pier and the Neva Gate became the second formal entrance into the fortress.

The side of the gate facing the river is decorated with a portico in the style of Classicism and four columns joined in pairs at the bottom by mighty granite blocks. The gate is crowned by a triangular pediment with images of an anchor placed on crossed branches and two bombs. Under the pediment is the inscription: *The Neva Gate, 1787.*

On the bastions facing the river the oldest surviving St Petersburg memorial inscriptions can be found. These inscriptions, executed in bronze letters, are fastened to granite slabs and indicate the dates when the granite reveting of the various bastions was completed. To give the inscriptions an even more solemn appearance, in several places the Cyrillic letter *H* is replaced with the Latin *N*.

The first two inscriptions of this type appeared on the faces of the bastion known today as the Naryshkin Bastion. Their identical text reads: "The Bastion of the Empress Catherine Alexeyevna. Clad in stone during the reign of Catherine II in 1870."

And it was from these very inscriptions that the title *Clad in Stone* was chosen by the eminent Soviet writer Olga Forsh for her novel

The Neva Gate from the Neva side and the Neva pier

written in 1924—25 and dedicated to the tragic fate of the "Russian Iron-Mask" — the nobleman-revolutionary Mikhail Beideman. Beideman emigrated to Italy in 1860 and fought for Risorgimento (the Union of Italy) in the detachment of Giuseppe Garibaldi. In 1861 he was arrested on the border attempting to return to his homeland, and was held without trial for twenty years in solitary confinement in the Secret House of the St Alexei Ravelin, where he went insane.

The novel *Clad in Stone* is the best among the literary works whose action takes place, at least partially, within the Peter and Paul Fortress. The latter was also the setting for scenes in the interesting film *The Palace and the Fortress*, first released in 1924, and whose script was written by Olga Forsh together with a former prisoner of the fortress, the historian and literary critic Piotr Shchogolev.

From the Neva pier the viewer may walk along the Neva Curtain Wall and the Tsar Bastion to the batardeau connecting the point of the latter with the half-counterguard covering its left face. In the batardeau the tops of two bricked-in arches mark the place where the aquatic gates were formerly located.

Walking further along the shore of the island one will soon see the St John Bridge and crossing the Kronwerk Strait over it, one will again be at the intersection of Kirov Prospekt and Kuibyshev Street.

The fortress today

After viewing the sights of Hare Island, one may take a short walk along the right shore of the Kronwerk Strait in the direction of the Defence Arsenal which stands opposite the Golovkin Bastion. The arsenal is a massive red-brick building (472 metres in length at its axis) reminiscent of a medieval Western European castle. The path to the arsenal leads across a small granite bridge suspended over the narrow moat to the right of the Kronwerk Strait. A low rampart runs along the left bank of the moat — all that remains of the walls of the kronwerk. The rampart and moat surround the arsenal on the east, north and west. A wrought-iron fence with street-lights begins immediately beyond the bridge and runs up to the eastern gate of the arsenal.

Not far from the bridge, beyond the fence, at the end of the kronwerk rampart, stands an obelisk of light granite erected in 1976. It bears a round metal bas-relief with the portrait profiles of the five leaders of the Decembrist Uprising of 1825 and below it the inscription: "On this spot on July 13—25, 1826, the Decembrists Pavel Pestel, Konstantin Ryleyev, Piotr Kakhovsky, Sergei Muravyov-Apostol and Mikhail Bestuzhev-Riumin were executed." The opposite side of the obelisk bears a few lines of verse, extraordinarily popular among Russian revolutionaries, written by the great Russian poet Alexander Pushkin in 1818 and sent to his friend Piotr Chaadayev:

Dear friend, have faith: the wakeful skies
Presage a dawn of wonder — Russia
Shall from her age-old sleep arise,
And despotism, impatient, crushing,
Upon its ruins our names incise!

(*Translated by Irina Zheleznova*)

In front of the obelisk on a low granite slab are the images of an officer's sword and broken chain symbolizing the revolt of progressively-minded Russian officers against despotism.

embrasure — a relatively wide opening in the wall of a permanent fortified structure through which guns are fired

gorge wall — the wall of a bastion or similar structure which joins two flanks

The eastern gate of the Defence Arsenal

This monument was installed by the citizens of Leningrad to commemorate the 150th anniversary of the Decembrist Uprising.

Proceeding along the iron fence with street lamps one will soon be at the eastern gates of the three-storey Defence Arsenal. Above the gate is the image of the Russian Imperial coat-of-arms, the monogram of Nicholas I — N I — with a crown and inscription "begun 1850", and the monogram of Alexander II — A II — with a crown and inscription "completed 1860" and the image of a bomb.

The ceremonial "laying of the cornerstone" on the already finished foundation and granite socle took place in 1851. The designers of the arsenal were Nicholas I and the eminent Russian military engineer Alexander Feldman; the building façades were designed by the architect P. Tamansky. The huge size of the building can be explained by the fact that it was intended "for the entire reserves of cold weapons and firearms to be held in St Petersburg, as well as field and siege artillery." Inasmuch as the building at the same time had significance in terms of defence, it was in essence a huge bastion, whose salient angle and shoulder corners were rounded. The exposed wall of the building has only embrasures, loopholes and united by a low stone gorge wall with gates, which separates the wide inner courtyard of the arsenal from the highway which runs along the bank of the strait.

The arsenal building now houses the Military-Historical Museum of Artillery, Engineering and Communication Forces. The museum exhibition is based on a collection organized in 1756 in the Liteiny House, the St Petersburg centre for artillery production, featuring "various experimental weapons and other curious and noteworthy items". On either side of the eastern gate of the arsenal stand two siege mortars used by the Russian army during

the Northern War in 1700—21; in the yard immediately before the gate eight captured European guns have been installed, and at the gate in the gorge wall there are eight Russian guns dating to the pre-revolutionary and early post-revolutionary periods. Besides the exhibits within the arsenal various examples of military hardware are on display in the arsenal courtyard as well.

In addition to the interesting authentic examples and models of Russian weaponry of the last six centuries, historical documents, banners, medals and photographs, the museum collection includes more than a few excellent works by the best Russian pre-revolutionary battle painters Bogdan (Gottfried) Willewalde, Nikolai Dmitriyev-Orenburgsky, Alexander Sauerweid, Alexei Kivshenko, Alexander von Kotzebue, Franz Roubaud, and others and by the eminent Soviet painters Mitrofan Grekov, Pavel Sokolov-Skalia and Vasily Yakovlev.

This concludes our tour of the Peter and Paul (St Petersburg) Fortress. We not only hope that with our help you have become better acquainted with the fortress than you were previously; but it is also our wish that you leave the fortress with a desire to find out still more about the interesting historical past and remarkable cultural wealth of the City on the Neva.

ПЕТРОПАВЛОВСКАЯ
(САНКТ-ПЕТЕРБУРГСКАЯ)
КРЕПОСТЬ

Историко-культурный путеводитель
(на английском языке)

Издательство „Аврора". Ленинград. 1989
Изд. № 2024. (2-20)
Типография ВО «Внешторгиздат», Москва
Printed and bound in the USSR